YORK MEDIEVAL TEXTS

General Editors

ELIZABETH SALTER & DEREK PEARSALL
University of York

Medieval English Lyrics

THEODORE SILVERSTEIN

Professor of English, University of Chicago

EDWARD ARNOLD

1975

First published 1971 by
Edward Arnold (Publishers) Ltd
41 Maddox Street, London W1

Cloth edition ISBN 07131 5559 0
Paper edition ISBN 07131 5560 4

Printed in Great Britain by
Billing & Sons Limited, Guildford and London

Preface

The present series of *York Medieval Texts* is designed for undergraduates and, where the text is appropriate, for upper forms of schools. Its aim is to provide editions of major pieces of Middle English writing in a form which will make them accessible without loss of historical authenticity. Texts are chosen because of their importance and artistic merit, and individual volumes may contain a single work, coherent extracts from a longer work, or representative examples of a genre. The principle governing the presentation of the text is to preserve the character of the English while eliminating unnecessary encumbrances such as obsolete letters. Glossary and explanatory notes operate together to clarify the text; special attention is paid to the interpretation of passages which are syntactically rather than lexically difficult. The introduction to each volume, like the rest of the apparatus, is designed to set the work in its proper literary context, and to provide the critical guidance most helpful to present-day readers.

This volume brings together a representative group of lyric poems written in the Middle English period. All but a few have been edited from the manuscripts and each is headed by a commentary which provides, not only standard references to earlier editions and listings, but also, as occasion suggests, a description of its character, its use of conventions and devices, its relation to other poems in the book. Many of the pieces were set to music in their time and where that music has survived and been made available in facsimile, printed form or the phonographic reproduction of a modern performance, the commentaries contain a note on the subject. Together with the general introduction, which asks in various ways what lyric poetry is, they focus the reader's attention, by both history and criticism, on the artistic qualities of the poems.

Contents

Introduction

THE lyrics in this book were written down between the opening of the thirteenth and the close of the fifteenth century. A few are no doubt a little later but in subject matter, manner, language and convention carry on the traditions of the previous time. This was the age of Chaucer, Lydgate, Hoccleve, at its latter end John Skelton, and of Robert Henryson, their lively fellow scribbler in Middle Scots; but none of their works appears in the following pages because in a small volume one must set a limit somewhere and the better known of these are often enough to be found in other collections. That still leaves a few remembered names among the one hundred and forty four poems which are included here: Friar William Herebert, Friar John Grimeston, the blind Shropshire poet John Awdelay, the carolist James Ryman, the elegant captive Frenchman (with a gift for English song) Charles duc d'Orléans and his well rehearsed but graver host the Duke of Suffolk, together with that rural though no less lovelorn gallant, Humfrey Newton Esquire of the Pownall Newtons, if indeed he made the various verses he records. The rest of the collection is anonymous (except for a pair of unconvincing Chaucer attributions), which means in fact most of it, and that is the natural condition of the body of the lyrics, including the finest among them, which survives from that period, to our pleasure.

No man likes another man's anthology, however he may dote upon his own. It can at least be said of the present one that it tries in little space to be as comprehensive as it can. Quality has, of course, been a prime consideration in the selection of the individual pieces, but so with one exception has been the representative character of the whole. The exception has to do with political songs, which this book has neglected entirely.

To contemplate the choices which both concerns together have dictated becomes, for editor and reader alike, an exercise in the principles of poetic and historical criticism. And the first literary problem that we face is to decide what a lyric poem is and in what sense or senses the poems set before us here are lyrics.

Though lyric poems have been written from early times, attempts to mark them off from other forms and to define them in their own variety are largely modern, nineteenth-century and twentieth indeed. The Hellenistic scholars of Alexandria who classified the body of traditional melic poetry, the words composed with song, of ancient Greece, did so by occasions, whether human or divine, together with the appropriate norms of genre and performance. Their accounts are thus material, conventional and technical, not formal in any stricter sense. Since then in the history of Western literary study many accounts have been produced of particular pieces according to theme, metrical pattern-

A*

ing, device; and anthologies have been arranged to reflect similar principles. The elaborate modern treatment by Herbert Weir Smyth to accompany his collection of Greek melic poetry, caps the very Alexandrians themselves in this mode. Greene's *Early English Carols*, a book of verses cited often in the present volume, prints them in groupings by their subjects—events in the life of Christ, the Virgin and certain saints—and for their order follows the occasions of the Christian year. To these he adds carols of secular interest, arranging them in two quite different categories, neither determined by a history or a calendar and each in turn different from the other: one is based on commonplace themes like marriage, love, mortality; and the other goes by purposes and ends—carols of moral counsel, convivial carols, political, satiric.

Not every verse collection need be systematic, simple convenience and a rough chronology may be enough; and this, on the whole, is how the present anthology is organized. But something might have been gained had we done it in the fashion of Smyth or Greene. To this we might have added, with complicating results, such other interests as social origins, anthropology, allegory and myth, which in our time have poked their way into criticism and collection: whether, for example, a piece is popular, even a remnant of folk custom, on the one hand, or learned or courtly, on the other; whether a poem belongs in the professional pack of the minstrel or comes from the private notebook of the amateur; or whether a song reflects traditional symbolisms or not. They are considerations of which some have affected the mixed bag of classifications in R. H. Robbins's well-known volume, *English Secular Lyrics of the XIVth and XVth Centuries*, and the learned journals are freighted with their consequences.

Much indeed would have been gained but there would also have been some things in danger of being lost, particularly such relevant considerations as, how from so limited a number of material subjects so large a body of poems is created, and how from but a single subject or *donnée*, let us say the Crucifixion, so moving a variety is formed. Questions such as these have to do with literary formation, not simply subject matter, social setting, origin, occasion; and the answer to them, as we scrutinize our choice of pieces, may lead us back by two different roads to the point where we began, asking what lyric poetry is and in what sense the poems in this book are lyrics.

The first road is a kind of historical criticism, the study of the presence in each poem of inherited traits of language, figure, genre and the rest, not for the sake of the history it discloses, but to place the poem where we can within its special milieu and its time; and more important, to discover how such traits are made to function as part of artistic construction, as well as what their role and power are in each instance. This notion of historical criticism is illustrated frequently in the commentaries which precede each text in the present volume.

Many of the poems to the Virgin, for example, which occur throughout the book, are basically rhetorical addresses filled out with the epithets of praise and blame, *de laudibus et vituperandis*, in keeping with the principles that came up in the schools from Roman times but also in the Christian line of Marian eulogy which established for the Middle Ages a common stock of terms, whether literally or by type, with which she might be lovingly described or desperately flattered, or hopefully. A parallel development of epithet and praise arises in poetic petitions by lover to his lady, and through being close in time and kind the two traditions co-mingle, so that the secular convention produces, with its formulas that raise a certain expectation, love epistles written to the Virgin.

Satire against women provided frequent opportunities for songs the strategies of which are rhetorical like those of addresses to the Virgin, but now of course *de vituperandis*. Here among a range of devices another figure plays its shaping role. This is the trope called by the rhetoricians *adynaton*, the postulating an object, condition or event impossible in nature. Lists of such *impossibilia* go back to Homer and the Bible and furnish a learned figure to the humanists of the Carolingian Renaissance and afterwards. The poet Walafrid Strabo gives us a classical instance of the trope, *Similitudo Impossibilium*, set down in Latin hexameters, which we render thus in rhymes as best we may:

A Posit of Impossibilities

Ravens white he'd have and swans like soot,
Slugs that talk in tongues and crickets mute;
Forbid the fish to swim and birds to fly;
Make fountains stand and mountains run, though dry,
And fire sink down and water rise on high;
Let bones with blood and nerves with marrow clot,
Stones grow soft but wax, when heated, not;
Get deer to crawl in dust, put snakes on legs;
Bid hens lay kids and goats give birth to eggs.

This is the figure pure without an application; in Poem 137 it becomes the premise of an argument, an *insinuatio* or argument indirect, the conclusion of which comes upon us strong, since unexpected:

When nettuls in wynter bryng forth rosys red
And al maner of thorn trys ber fygys naturally
And ges ber perles in euery med
And laurell ber cherys abundantly
And okys ber datys very plentuosly
And kyskys[1] gyfe of hony superfluens,
    Than put women in trust and confydens.

[1] 'Dry stalks'.

These sorts of combination are only a few of the ways by which a limited number of *données* were made to yield a fair variety of poems. The same is likewise true of other genres, both spiritual and secular, as they shape the verses we are here considering. Complaint, Nocturnal Vision and Lament are represented in exemplars by themselves alone and in union with each other, as in *Sodenly Afraide* (Poem 82) and in the *Canticus Amoris* (Poem 50), which also adds to its *mélange* the mystic love conventions deriving from the Song of Songs. In a recent study of the religious poetry of the period Rosemary Woolf has shown how the Crucifixion, traditionally a theme for contemplation, produced a body of poetic meditations comparable yet different to those of the seventeenth century. It also formed a basis, we may add, for wayside verse and graveyard verse and other common specimens of *Memento mori* (Poems 34, 44, 54, 55). At the other end of Jesus' life the happy theme of the Birth naturally draws to itself the jubilee, the lullaby, the ceremonial singsong of the Carol. And even the 'sinful' play of that secular genre, the Chanson d'Aventure (Poem 22), undergoes conversion to piety (Poem 27) and finds a charming echo in a carol for the Christmas season (Poem 92). Perhaps the greatest opportunity, however, for combination and invention is found by the poets in Nature and the Seasons, which variously subserve the joy, the pain, the yearning of love, both worldly and religious, and with the topos of the *cursus annorum*, that all too hurried passage of the years, the bitter sweet of death and mutability. The marks of such discovery appear throughout our book, where only *Svmer Is Icumen In* (Poem 17) gives us springtime's frisky joy without a single use or application.

Further devices of language or of statement often enough arise, not from the practices of rhetoric, but from poetic conventions proper and from song, as in the rondeaux of Charles duc d'Orléans (Poems 123, 124), the carols with their verses and obligatory burden, and the words and metaphors which are the common coinage of a well-developed courtly poetry. The music as well for which some of the verses were written makes up part of circumstance and history, moulding line and phrase to particular conformation.

All considerations such as these will take us along the road of time and milieu and bring us in sight of our poems' qualities, especially their medieval qualities, yet will not tell us how, distinct from other kinds, any of them, or none of them, are lyrics as poems of different times and places are lyrics. To deal with that nice problem we must walk the other road, which takes us back by way of a kind of formal criticism.

Modern critics seeking to define the lyric and to distinguish it from other forms have variously talked of its relation to song, its brevity, its intensity, its selection of significant moment rather than fuller narrative. A lyric is, as it were, short, sweet and meaningful. The term itself, lyric, recalling that Greek songs were once performed to the accompaniment of the lyre and in some way still implying a musical connection, will not in the end give us a definition; even a fragment of prose may be set to a tune, and during the three centuries represented by our medieval poems other kinds of verse, including long narratives, were made to be sung and were so performed. Many of the present poems were written for music, to be sure, and much of it survives, as the head commentaries in this volume frequently attest; many others, however, were not. Yet no one would doubt that these too, like countless later pieces never intended for musical performance, are also in a real sense lyrics.

Nor will brevity as a principle of definition unqualified get us very much further. An epigram may be as brief or briefer, and not every couplet is *per se* a lyric. Granted that the lyric belongs with the smaller forms of poetry, more limited than tragedy or epic or other kinds of narrative, how small and limited must it be? The verses in this book range in size between two lines and one hundred and eighty (Poem 76 and, in its uncut state, 47); Poems 1 and 2, both on the same subject, the Crucifixion and Compassion, are respectively a group of eleven six-line stanzas and a single quatrain made up of a pair of rhyming couplets, a proportion in their lengths of eleven to one.

But perhaps the critic may mean by brevity a concentration or intensity, whether intellectual, emotional or imaginative; if he does then he will be reminded that *King Lear* is as intense as any lyric and that any well-formed melodrama could be. On the other hand, we may readily observe how many poems in this volume are essentially plain straightforward statements, neat and rhythmic surely, but otherwise free of any special marks of concentration. Yet somewhere here there seems to lie a truth about the nature of the lyric that we cannot afford to overlook, and one of the ways to seek that truth is to examine particular instances of poetic concentration forced by a principle of brevity, in order to see how far that principle can be specified and found to be basic to a kind. Let us look with this in mind at Poems 2, 8, 18 and 19, one on the Crucifixion, one on mortality, and two on love.

Poem 2, *Ci doit tu penser de la duce Marie*, is one of the earliest and certainly the loveliest of the fifteen or eighteen pieces in the book having as their common theme the Crucifixion and Passion, each different, sometimes subtly different, from the others. It is also the shortest among them:

> Nou goth sonne vnder wode;
> Me rewes, Marie, thi faire rode.
> Nou goth sonne vnder tre;
> Me rewes, Marie, thi sone and the.

As in Poems 1, 3 and 4 the Virgin in it stands near the centre of the scene, but a scene from which now are removed the usual details of cross, torment, noisy crowd of human actors, and the time-span of which is compressed into almost a single moment. All that is left are Mary and Jesus; the sun below woods and tree (if not by another reading simply tree), making them rise up to the speaker's horizon in a narrowing, specifying focus; and the direct statement of the speaker's emotion. The two sets of lines, 1, 3 and 2, 4, the first describing things seen and the other the feeling, operate in brief like incremental repetition in a ballad, an iteration of something already said with a small progressive change; but this alone is merely a device of disclosure. The basic quality of the poem lies in its method of abstraction, saying less than the reader knows about the events involved, hence suggesting more than is said, so that sunset, woods, tree become a kind of symbolic shorthand which brings recognition, including a sense of quiet not mentioned otherwise, and by such indirection sharpens the image and deepens the emotion even as its statement is simplified and made gentle.

Poems 8, 18 and 19, all of them equally brief, move us by comparable kinds of symbolic shorthand. In Poem 8, *Wen the Turuf Is Thi Tuur*, secular weal and death are placed in simple offset in two sets of figural abstractions from the fuller worlds which they represent:

> Wen the turuf is thi tuur
> And thi put[1] is thi bour,
> Thi wel[2] and thi wite throte
> Ssulen wormes tonote[3]
> Wat helpit the thenne
> Al the worilde wnne[4]

The argument moves by metaphor and analogy, merging the two contrasted states, a *concors discordantium* of the present and the future, into an imaginative now, which also like the now of Poem 2 shifts us to a limiting focus, from spacious world to small oppressive grave, and the plain rhetorical question that follows as both climax and conclusion makes the emotion immediate. *The story, my proud fellow, is of thee!* Poems 18 and 19 are love songs which bring us summer and winter as loci for longing and care. Birds and fish and flood and night and winter's blast, the shorthand of these pieces, are commonplace like woods and tree and tower and bower and worms—nothing could be more commonplace—yet disciplined as the latter are by tradition to create the lover's special world and intensify, by a similitude or contrast of which he is aware, the dilemma in which he finds himself.

All four of these poems are examples of what we recognize as a lyric intensity forced by brevity of a particular kind. There are many other kinds but we need not follow their divergent traces here. Sometimes brevity is not a world

---

[1] 'Pit'.   [2] 'Skin'.   [3] 'Gnaw up'.   [4] 'Profit'.

compressed into an image or emotion, but a brevity of play and even cere-monial. For if, as Polonius tells us, brevity is the soul of wit, wit may be the soul of brevity. Not epigram, for that is not the brevity we seek, but a song which lives in a turn of humour and of grace, as in *My Ghostly Fadir* by that light-tongued singer Charles d'Orléans (Poem 124), which confesses to a lover's sin and vows to set it right ('I stole a kiss, Father, I'll return it if I can'); or that capsule history of man, delightful as a piece of wit, *Adam Lay Iboundyn* (Poem 80) (If Adam hadn't eaten the apple and so bound us all in sin, we wouldn't have had Our Blessed Lady as Queen of Heaven. *O felix culpa!*). As for ceremonial, many a carol on drinking or eating proceeds by the rhetoric of specifying and listing and by argument *ex contrariis;* for example, *Bryng Vs in Good Ale* (Poem 133):

> Bryng vs in no browne bred fore that is mad of brane,
> Nor bryng vs in no whyt bred fore therin is no game,
> But bryng vs in good ale.

> Bryng vs in no befe for ther is many bonys,
> But bryng vs in good ale for that goth downe at onys,
> And bryng vs in good ale.

No one would take such names and lists as a catalogue of foods, a culinary treatise or an argument for drink. Carols are typically short and ceremonial, their occasions are often those of festival and play. Their burden's marked rhythm and iteration are frequently enough made to produce a comedy, the basis of which lies in a jovial group performance, underlined and repeated—as in that carol against women, not included in the present volume, where verses of apparently serious praise are perverted by the swelling joyous accent of its all male burden:

> Of all Creatures women be best:
> Cuius contrarium verum est.

Finally, though the boundaries of lyric brevity will hardly have been reached, there is the brevity of what may be called the plain style, the best examples of which are found in simple prayers. The plain style, said St. Augus-tine, is that with which to expound the truth of Scripture; but the highest form of rhetoric, overgoing Cicero's, said Roger Bacon, are Christian works of prayer and devotion. If that is the most elevated of literature it is an elevation residing in the sublimity of occasion and the intensity of poetic formation rather than in style or words. Not necessarily imagistic or abstracting like the four poems we considered on the Crucifixion, mortality and love, such a prayer may use language that is commonplace and statement that is simpler in arrangement than theirs. Poem 11, *A, Iesu Crist That Ous Is Boue*, and Poem 88, *Vpon My Ryght Syde Y Me Leye*, are perhaps the two most touching specimens in the book of this sort of lyric brevity.

Brevity may therefore show itself in length, concentration, abstraction, form of statement. But what stands behind these varieties that makes them valid as lyric? That they are the expression of a speaker, not necessarily the thoughts or feelings of the poet, rather the 'I' who with us talks of his response to some condition or event. In a recent essay Elder Olson[1] has sought to get at the character of the lyric generally by describing its action and actor:

> The peculiar nature of lyric poetry is related, not to its verbal brevity, but to the brevity of the human behaviour which it depicts. Its verbal brevity, in general, is a consequence of the brevity of its action. The larger forms are impossible without extensive actions. . . . An extended action is likely to require a certain number of characters. . . . On the other hand, the most common forms of lyric show us a single character behaving in some manner in a single situation—sometimes even a single moment; it is impossible to imagine anything smaller than *that*.
>
> Moreover, the larger forms exhibit the changing *fortunes* of their characters, in relation to their behaviour. The lyric does not exhibit the *changes* of fortune. . . . The larger forms, too, are primarily concerned with *interpersonal* action . . . since changes in fortune chiefly come about through actions which involve others. The lyric is concerned, primarily with *personal* action or reaction as such; that is, with how some individual feels or thinks or acts in a given situation; it is concerned with that behaviour in isolation, without reference to its position in a sequence of incidents.

For dealing strictly with the problem of definition this rather Aristotelian description of the lyric as the expression of a limited human action will seem to have a special value, even where the 'I' in question speaks with the voice of the community or the 'behaviour' is essentially an internal state of being. There are other ways, however, of looking at the lyric and each way depends on the particular end in view. Christian worship can be seen as a little drama, but since prayers are panegyrics or persuasions it is also enlightening, with Friar Bacon, to consider them in terms of an appropriate rhetoric, in which 'thou' or 'you' becomes a major consideration of person, just as their emotional quality may suggest the aptness of a psychological interest and their imaginative rise the relevance of a Coleridgean poetics. To try the pieces in this volume from various points of view would be to exercise the critical judgment itself and, beyond the search for definition, to test the practical use of each view for the reading of any single poem.

[1] 'The Lyric', *Papers of the Midwest Modern Language Association* 1 (1969), pp. 59–66.

The texts which follow, except for a dozen or so, have been freshly edited directly from the manuscripts. In some cases that has meant a considerable deviation from the previously accepted readings; the textual notes and occasionally the commentaries record the chief instances. The original spelling in its complex kinds is left inviolate throughout but graphics are modernized, as are often line divisions. Titles are frequently the editor's.

Perhaps the greatest innovation in the book affects chronology, which is very rough and sketchy at best and remains a problem for all students of the period. Carleton Brown and others have tended to see in such fourteenth-century collections as the Harley Lyrics pieces of a much earlier origin. Further study tends to place them ever later than was thought; the Harley Lyrics in this volume have been shifted to the fourteenth century, which leaves, we fear, very little for the thirteenth. At the other end, however, generosity has prevailed. Humfrey Newton's poems and certain others are surely early sixteenth century. The excuse for their inclusion is made at the beginning of this introduction, and so the argument comes full circle.

Si tibi placet

Books for Consultation and Further Reading

Note: Abbreviations used throughout this volume are given here in square brackets.

I WORKS CITED FREQUENTLY IN COMMENTARY

A *Texts and MSS*

1 [*Index*] Carleton Brown and R. H. Robbins, *The Index of Middle English Verse* (New York 1943). With list of MSS.

2 [*Supplement*] R. H. Robbins and J. L. Cutler, *Supplement to the Index of Middle English Verse* (University of Kentucky Press 1965).

3 [Walther, *Initia*] Hans Walther, *Initia Carminum ac Versuum Medii Aevi Posterioris Latinorum* (Göttingen 1959). This book and 4 below record the body of medieval Latin poems and proverbs, many related to the English.

4 [Walther, *Sprichwörter*] Hans Walther, *Proverbia Sententiaeque Latinitatis Medii Aevi* (Gottingen 1963–67). 5 volumes.

5 [Mone] *Lateinische Hymnen des Mittelalters* edited by F. J. Mone (Freiburg im Breisgau 1853; reprinted 1964). 3 volumes. A standard edition of the Christian Latin hymns.

6 [Brown *XIII*] *English Lyrics of the XIIIth Century* edited by Carleton Brown (Oxford 1932). This and 7–12 below are standard editions, with reference in their notes to earlier editions.

7 [Brown *XIV*] *Religious Lyrics of the XIVth Century* edited by Carleton Brown (second, revised edition, G. V. Smithers, Oxford 1957).

8 [Robbins *Sec. XIV–XV*] *Secular Lyrics of the XIVth and XVth Centuries* edited by R. H. Robbins (second edition, Oxford 1955, reprinted 1961).

9 [Brown *XV*] *Religious Lyrics of the XVth Century* edited by Carleton Brown (Oxford 1939; reprinted 1962).

10 [EETS 255] *Facsimile of British Museum MS Harley 2253* with an introduction by N. R. Ker (Early English Text Society 255, 1965 for 1964).

11 [Brook] *The Harley Lyrics: The Middle English Lyrics of MS Harley 2253* edited by G. L. Brook (Manchester University Press, third edition 1964).

12 [Greene] *The Early English Carols* edited by R. L. Greene (Oxford 1935).

13 R. H. Robbins, 'The Poems of Humfry Newton, Esquire, 1466–1536', *PMLA* LXV (1950), pp. 249–81.

14 R. H. Robbins, 'The Findern Anthology', *PMLA* LXIX (1954), pp. 610–42.

B *Music*

15 [Stainer] *Early Bodleian Music* edited by Sir John Stainer, with an intro-

duction by E. W. B. Nicholson and transcriptions by J. F. R. and C. Stainer (London and New York 1910). 2 volumes.

16 [Harrison] Frank Ll. Harrison, *Music in Medieval Britain* (London 1958).

17 [Argo Record RG 443] *Medieval English Lyrics* with notes on texts by E. J. Dobson and on music by F. Ll. Harrison (London 1965). A singing performance of Poems 1, 10, 17, 18 and 19.

C   *History and Criticism*

18 [Woolf] Rosemary Woolf, *The English Religious Lyric in the Middle Ages* (Oxford 1968).

II   OTHER WORKS

A   *Texts*

19 *Early English Lyrics* chosen by Frank Sidgwick and E. K. Chambers (London 1907; new edition 1966).

20 *Cambridge Middle English Lyrics* edited by H. A. Person (University of Washington Press, Seattle, 1962).

21 *The Advent Lyrics of the Exeter Book* edited by Jackson J. Campbell (Princeton University Press 1959).

22 *Early Middle English Verse and Prose* edited by J. A. W. Bennett and G. V. Smithers, with a glossary by Norman Davis (second edition, Oxford 1968). Section VIII prints some lyrics and pp. 316–36 offer a commentary.

B   *History and Criticism*

23 Peter Dronke, *Medieval Latin and the Rise of the European Love-Lyric* Oxford 1965). 2 volumes. The Harley lyrics are discussed in I, pp. 112–25.

24 Peter Dronke, *The Medieval Lyric* (London 1968). European in range; early English, pp. 63–70.

25 Elder Olson, 'Introduction' to *American Lyric Poems from Colonial Times to the Present* (New York 1964). This book and *26* below address critically the problem of definitions and forms.

26 Elder Olson, 'The Lyric', *Papers of the Midwest Modern Language Association* 1 (1969), pp. 59–66.

27 Theodore Silverstein, 'The Art of Sir Gawain and the Green Knight', *University of Toronto Quarterly* XXXIII (1964), pp. 258–78. Touches on lyric conventions, devices and language, in the fourteenth and fifteenth centuries.

28 Herbert Weir Smyth, *Greek Melic Poets* (New York and London 1900; reprinted 1963). Introduction classifies traditional songs.

Religious and Moral Poems
of the Thirteenth Century

1   *Chauncoun de Nostre Dame*   Early 13 c.

Based generally on the *Stabat iuxta Christi Crucem*, this poem is related music-ally and in stanza pattern to several 13 c. English translations of that hymn: *cf* Poem 4 and Brown *XIII*, 4, and see Woolf, pp. 243–6 and Harrison, pp. 153–5. The contrast between the external pain of Jesus and Mary's internal suffering is also the Latin hymn's theme, but the English development as a dramatic dialogue is its own.

BM MS Royal 12 E. 1, ff. 193–94ᵛ. Index 3211. Brown XIII, 49B. The French title from version in Bodl, MS Digby 86 , f. 127, col. 1. For music hear Argo Record RG 443, item 8.

> 'Stand wel, moder, vnder rode,
> Bihold thi child wyth glade mode;
> Blythe, moder, mittu ben.'
> 'Svne, quu may y blithe stonden?
> Hi se thin feet, hi se thin honden   5
> Nayled to the harde tre.'
>
> 'Moder, do wey thi wepinge;
> Hi thole this ded for mannes thinge;
> For owen gilte tholi non.'
> 'Svne, hi fele the dede stunde;   10
> The swerd is at min herte grunde
> That me byhytte Symeon.'
>
> 'Moder, reu vpon thi bern;
> Thu wasse awey tho blodi teren,
> It don me werse than mi ded.'   15
> 'Sune, hu mitti teres wernen?
> Hy se tho blodi flodes hernen
> Huth of thin herte to min fet.'

4. y: *supplied*

'Moder, nu y may the seyn
Better is that ic one deye   20
Than al mankyn to helle go.'
'Sune, y se thi bodi swngen,
Thi brest, thin hond, thi fot thurstungen;
No selli thou me be wo.'

'Moder, if y dar the tellen   25
Yif y ne deye thu gost to helle;
Hi thole this ded for thine sake.'
'Sune, thu best me so minde,
Ne with me nout; it is mi kinde
That y for the sorye make.'   30

'Moder, merci, let me deyen
For Adam ut of helle beyn
And al mankin that is forloren.'
'Sune, wat sal me to rede?
Thi pine pined me to dede;   35
Let me deyn the biforen.'

'Moder, mitarst thu mith leren
Wat pine tholen that childre beren,
Wat sorwe hauen that child forgon.'
'Sune, y wot y kan the tellen   40
Bute it be the pine of helle
More sorwe ne woth y non.'

'Moder, reu of wymanes kare
Nu thu wost of moder fare,
Thou thu be clene mayden man.'   45

29. Ne: *supplied*
43. wymanes: MS moder
45. man: an *supplied: leaf torn, with end of this and following lines missing*

---

34. *wat . . . rede:* 'what shall be as counsel for me', i.e. 'what shall I do?'
43-4. 'Mother, have pity on women's troubles now thou knowest about a mother's state'

'Sune, help alle at nede,
Alle tho that to me greden,
Mayden, wyf and fol wyman.'

'Moder, y may no lenger duellen,
The time is cumen y fare to helle;   50
The thridde day y rise upon.'
'Sune, y wyle wi'the funden.
Y deye ywis of thine wnden,
So reuful ded was neuere non.'

When he ros than fel thi sorwe,   55
The blisse sprong the thridde morwe
When blithe moder were thu tho.
Moder, for that ilke blisse
Bisech vre God vre sinnes lesse;
Thu be hure chel ayen hure fo.   60

Blisced be thu, quen of heuene,
Bring us ut of helle leuene
Thurth thi dere sunes mith.
Moder, for that hithe blode
That he sadde vpon the rode   65
Led us into heuene lith.   Amen.

2   *Ci Doit Tu Penser de la*   Early 13 c.
                    Duce Marie

This poem occurs in St. Edmund of Pontigny, *Speculum Ecclesie*, in the medi-
tation on the Passion for sext at the Virgin's commitment to St. John at the
Cross and is preceded by a French rhythmical piece: see H. W. Robbins, *Le*

48. mayden: ay *supplied*   49. lenger: *supplied*
51. thridde day: *supplied*   53. deye ywis: *supplied*
54. neuere non: MS neue   55. When: *supplied*
56. sprong ... morewe: MS spr   58. Moder ... blisse: MS mod

60. 'Be thou our shield against our foe'

Merure de Seinte Eglise by Saint Edmund of Pontigny (Lewisburg, Penn., 1925),
p. 63. 'Wode' may be 'woods' or 'wood' and in the latter case signifies,
together with 'tre', the Cross. The French quotation of *Ruth* I. 20 and *Cant.* I.
15, together with the medieval commentaries explaining that Mary's face is
black from suffering, annotate the reference to her countenance in lines 1 and
2. For those who like to find 'correspondences' everywhere the sunset will be
an obvious figure for Christ's death.

Comparison of this poem with the 16 c. quatrain *O westron wind* is common-
place and rests on the observation that each uses a single moment among an
elaborate series of events both to suggest them and to distil from them a
particular lyric emotion. The present poem depends on the reader's knowledge
of the Passion traditions, especially the accounts of Mary at the Cross, e.g.
in Poems 1 and 3; but it picks the quiet moment at sunset to state its compassion.
For contrasting uses of the quiet moment see Old English *Dream of the Rood*,
and Poem 45. (See also introduction, pp. 5 and 6.)

*Bodl. MS Digby 20, ff. 154ᵛ–55. Index 2320. Brown XIII, 1. Title from French
passage preceding English quatrain in MS.*

> Nou goth sonne vnder wode;
> Me rewes, Marie, thi faire rode.
> Nou goth sonne vnder tre;
> Me rewes, Marie, thi sone and the.

3   *On Leome Is in This World Ilist*   Before mid 13 c.

For similar descriptions of the physical torments of Jesus, characteristic of all
such poems on the Passion, *cf* Poems 1, 4, 5, 12, 45, etc.

*Camb. Trinity Coll. MS 323, ff. 32ᵛ, col. 1–33, col. 2 (with omissions as indicated
by series of points). Index 293. Brown XIII, 24.*

> On leome is in this world ilist,
> Therof is muchel pris;
> Arisen is God and that is rist
> From dethe to lif.
> Al for ure redempciun   5
> He tholede pine and passiun,
> Derne wnden and greve;
> He broutte to saluaciun

The world that was ibrot adun
Thuru Adam and Eue. . . .   10

His bodi that wes feir and gent
And his neb suo scene
Wes bispit and al torend,
His rude wes worthen grene.
Bufetes him weren iyeuene;   15
Of serue ther wes euene
Tho he bigon to bleden.
He bahit wid milde steuene
Then suete feder of heuene
Firyewen hem heore misdeden. . . .   20

Hasse he biheuld the rode,
The modir that was of miste
And ther isei al ablode
Hir sone that her wes briste,
Hisse tuo suete honden   25
Wid nailes al toronden,
Is fehit ithurlid bo,
Is suete softe side
Ithurlit depe and wyde—
Wey, that hire was wo!   30

Ha isei the rode stonden,
Hire sone therto ibunden,
Hoe wroinc hire honden,
Biheild his suete wunden.
The Gyues to him leden   35
On him forto greden
Asse that hoe weren wod.
Hire thucte a miste aweden,
Hire herte bigon to bleden,
Teres hoe wep of blod.   40

15. MS iþeuene

---

35. *Gyues:* 'Jews'

Lauedi, flur of parradis
(Nas neuir non so scene),
Ber hure herrinde if thi vil his,
Asse thu ard heuene quene,
To thine sone that is so brit,   45
That he us yeue strenthe and mist
To seruen him wid wunne,
And to scenden thene vichit
That his humbe day and nicst
To gabben us wid sunne. . . .   50

4   *Biheld Hire Sone o Rode*   Mid 13 c.

   A translation of the Latin hymn *Stabat iuxta Christi Crucem* but with the
introduction of an 'I' speaker, whose responses serve as a simple device to
make the Virgin's experience more moving and relevant: see Poem 1 above
and its commentary, and Brown *XIII*, 4, with its similar 'I' speaker and his
prayer at the end. *Cf* also Poems 5 and 9 and their commentaries.

*BM MS Arundel 248, ff. 154ᵛ–55. Index 1697. Brown XIII, 47. For the Latin,
Walther, Initia 18575.*

            Iesu Cristes milde moder
            Stud, biheld hire sone o rode
            That he was ipined on.
            The sone heng, the moder stud
            And biheld hire childes blud   5
            Wu it of hise wundes ran.

            Tho he starf that king is of lif,
            Dreriere nas neuerre no wif
            Than thu were, leuedi, tho.
            The brithe day went into nith   10
            Tho Ihesu Crist, thin herte lith,

46. MS þeue

_____

48. *vichit = wiht*: 'creature', i.e. the Devil
11. thin: MS hin

Was iqueint with pine and wo.

Thi lif drei ful harde stundes
Tho thu seye hise bludi wundes
And his bodi o rode don.   15
Hise wundes sore and smerte
Stungen thureu and thurw thi herte
As te bihichte Simeon.

Nu his heued with blud bisprunken,
Nu his side with spere istungen   20
Thu bihelde, leuedi fre;
Nu his hondes sprad o rode,
Nu hise fet washen wit blode
An inaillet to the tre.

Nu his bodi with scurges beten   25
And his blud so wide hutleten
Maden the thin herte sor.
Warso thu castest thin eyen,
Pine strong thu soie im dreien,
Ne mithte noman tholie more.   30

Nu is time that thu yielde
Kende that thu im withelde
Tho thi child was of the born.
Nu he hoschet with goulinge
That thu im in thi chiltinge   35
Al withelde thar biforn.

Nu thu fondest, moder milde,
Wat wyman drith with hir childe,
Thei thu clene maiden be.
Nu the's yiolden arde and dere   40
The pine werof thu were
Ine ti chilthing quite and fre.

31. MS þielde   **40.** MS þiolden

Sone after the nith of sorwen
Sprong the lith of edi morwen;
Ine thin herte, suete may,   45
Thi sorwen wende al to blisse
Tho thi sone al mid iwisse
Aros hupon the tridde day.

Welle wat thu were blithe
Tho ha ros fram deth to liue,   50
Thur the hole ston he glod.
Al so he was of the boren,
Bothen after and biforen
Hol bilof thi maidenhod.

Neu blisse he us broute   55
That mankin so dere boute
And for us yaf is dere lif.
Glade and blithe thu us make
For thi suete sones sake,
Edi maiden, blisful wif.   60

Quen of euene, for thi blisse
Lithe al hure sorinesse
And went hur yuel al into gud.
Bring hus, moder, to thi sone,
Mak hus eure with im wone   65
That hus boute wit his blud.

                              Amen.

5   *The Minde of Thi Passiun*   13 c.

A poem on the Passion, the words of which, those of an implied speaker
engaged in meditation, effect a concentration on the vision of Christ's torments
themselves. *Cf* Poem 14 and Brown *XIII*, 34–37 (the last written on the verso

---

50. *Or* h'aros: MS þaros   **51, 52, 55.** he: MS þe   **57.** MS þaf

of the present poem's folio), in which the introduction of an explicit 'I', whatever its virtues, modifies the imaginative focus.

Bodl. MS Ashmole 360, f. 145, col. 1. Index 1977. Brown XIII, 56A.

> *Memoria passionis tue, O bone Ihesu,*
> *Lacrimas tollit,*
> *Oculos effundit,*
> *Faciem humectat,*
> *Cor dulcorat.*   5

> The minde of thi passiun, suete Ihesu,
> The teres it tollid,
> The heine it bolled,
> The neb it wetth,
> In herte sueteth.   10

6   *Sunt Tria Que Vere Faciunt*   Mid 13 c.
                  Me Sepe Dolere

For the various versions and related pieces, Latin and English, see Brown's Notes to *XIII*, 11 and 12, and *cf* Poems 30, line 15; 33, lines 15–16; and 46, lines 22–4 and 33–6.

Oxf. Jesus Coll. MS 29, f. 189. Index 695. Brown XIII 11B. The Latin text and title from MS Ashmole 1393, f. 51ᵛ. Walther Initia 18886.

> *Sunt tria que vere faciunt me sepe dolere:*
> *Est primum durum quia scio me moriturum,*
> *Secundum timeo quia tempus nescio quando,*
> *Unde magis flebo quia nescio quo remanebo.*

> Yche day me cumeth tydinges threo   5
> For wel swithe sore beoth heo:
> The on is that ich schal heonne,
> That other that ich noth hwenne;
> The thridde is my meste kare,
> That ich not hwider ich scal fare.   10

7   *Memorare Novissima Tua*   Mid 13 c.

This homiletic poem, which refers to the practice of removing the body at
death from bed to floor and thence to the grave, occurs in a variety of forms
from the 13 to 16 c., and becomes associated with pieces on the signs of
approaching death: *cf* the Notes to Brown *XIII*, 13 and 71 and the text of 71,
and Walther *Initia* 17947.

BM MS Arundel 292, f. 3ᵛ. Index 1422. Brown XIII, 13.

If man him bithocte
Inderlike and ofte
Wu arde is te fore
Fro bedde te flore,
Wu reuful is te flitte   5
Fro flore to pitte,
Fro pitte te pine
That neure sal fine,
I wene non sinne
Sulde his herte winnen.   10

8   *Wen the Turuf Is Thi Tuur*   Mid 13 c. or after

See introduction, p. 6.

Camb. Trin. Coll. MS 323, f. 47ᵛ. Index 4044. Brown XIII, 30.

Cum sit gleba tibi turris,
Tuus puteus conclauis,
Pellis et guttur album
Erit cibus vermium,
Quid habent tunc de proprio   5
Hii monarchie lucro?

Vnde Anglice sic dicitur:

Wen the turuf is thi tuur
And thi put is thi bour,
Thi wel and thi wite throte   10
Ssulen wormes tonote,
Wat helpit the thenne
Al the worilde wnne?

Of On That Is So Fayr and Briht   Mid 13 c. or after

This macaronic poem, at once the cry of a penitent for succour and a praise
of the Virgin, is related in character and stanza form to Brown *XIII*, 16, and
appears with it in another version (Brown, 17A) in Camb. Trin. Coll. MS 323,
f. 24ᵛ. Both poems are connected to Latin models of Marian eulogy and in
at least one instance (MS Rawl. C504) the present piece appears among a group
of Latin hymns: R. W. Hunt, in *Mediaeval and Renaissance Studies* V (1961),
p. 34; but the personal appeals of the 'I' speaker are, again, peculiar to the
English: *cf* Poems 4 and 5 and their commentaries.

BM MS Egerton 613, f. 2. Index 2645. Brown XIII, 17B.

Of on that is so fayr and briht
Velud maris stella,
Brihter than the dayis liht,
Parens et puella,
Ic crie to the, thou se to me,   5
Leuedy, preye thi sone for me
Tam pia,
That ic mote come to the,
Maria.

Leuedi, flour of alle thing,   10
Rosa sine spina,
Thou bere Ihesu, heuene king,
Gratia diuina.
Of alle thou berst the pris,
Leuedi, quene of parays   15
Electa;
Mayde milde moder es
Effecta.

Al this world was forlore,
Eua peccatrice,   20
Tyl our lord was ybore
De te genitrice.

MS *gives stanzas in this order: 1, 3, 2, 5, 4, but with indications that the order is to be
rearranged.*

With aue it went away
Thuster nyth and comet the day
Salutis.   25
The welle springet hut of the
Virtutis.

Wel he wot he is thi sone
Ventre quem portasti;
He wyl nout werne the thi bone   30
Paruum quem lactasti.
So hende and so god he his,
He hauet brout ous to blis
Superni,
That hauet hidut the foule put   35
Inferni.

Of kare conseil thou ert best,
Felix fecundata;
Of alle wery thou ert rest,
Mater honorata.   40
Bisek him wit milde mod
That for ous alle sad is blod
In cruce,
That we moten komen til him
In luce.   45

Explicit cantus iste.

10   *Edi Beo Thu, Heuene Quene*   Mid 13 c.

   A prayer to the Virgin uniting the conventions of religious supplication
with those of knightly devotion from secular poetry, which in turn had brought
religious terminology to its celebration of worldly love. Like all prayers which
are also songs of praise flattering to the divinity addressed, this piece is made
up of standard figures, in the present instance from Marian eulogy, including
the figure of the shield against Hell-pain: *cf* e.g. lines 1–2, and generally, with
Mone, II, 210; lines 9–12 with Chevalier, 1620 ('Aurora caeli praevia / a nocte
lucem separat'), and with Poem 3, line 1; lines 25–32 with Poem 79; and see

Poem 28. See also Poem 27, similar in mixture though otherwise differently formed.

Dobson, Notes to Argo 443, argues that the text, though readable, is corrupt and emends to make it better suit the music.

Oxf. Corpus Christi Coll. MS E 59, f. 113ᵛ. Index 708. Brown XIII, 60. For music hear Argo Record RG 443, item 3.

Edi beo thu, Heuene Quene,
Folkes froure and engles blis,
Moder unwemmed and maiden clene,
Swich in world non other nis.
On the hit is wel eth sene   5
Of alle wimmen thu hauest thet pris.
Mi swete leuedi, her mi bene
And reu of me yif thi wille is.

Thu asteye so the daiyrewe
The deleth from the deorke nicht,   10
Of the sprong a leome newe
That al this world haueth ilicht.
Nis non maide of thine heowe
Swo fair, so sschene, so rudi, swo bricht.
Swete leuedi, of me thu reowe   15
And haue merci of thin knicht.

Spronge blostme of one rote,
The holi gost the reste upon;
Thet wes for monkunnes bote
And heore soule to alesen for on.   20
Leuedi milde, softe and swote,
Ic crie the merci, ic am thi mon
Bothe to honde and to fote
On alle wise that ic kon.

Thu ert eorthe to gode sede,   25
On the lichte the heouene deuw,
Of the sprong theo edi blede,
The holi gost hire on the seuw.

Thu bring us ut of kare of drede
That Eue bitterliche us breuw, 30
Thu sschalt us into heouene lede:
Welle swete is the ilke deuw.

Moder ful of thewes hende,
Maide dreich and wel itaucht,
Ic em in thin loue bende 35
And to the is al mi draucht.
Thu me sschilde from the feonde
Ase thu ert freo and wilt and maucht,
Help me to mi liues ende
And make me with thin sone isaucht. 40

Thu ert icumen of heye kunne
Of Dauid the riche king.
Nis non maiden under sunne
The mei beo thin euening
Ne that swo derne louiye kunne 45
Ne non swo treowe of alle thing.
Thi loue us brouchte eche wunne,
Ihered ibeo thu, swete thing.

Seolcuthliche ure louerd hit dichte
That thu, maide withute were, 50
That al this world bicluppe ne michte
Sscholdest of thin boseme bere.
The ne stichte ne the ne prichte
In side, in lende, ne elleswhere;
That wes with muchel richte 55
For thu bere thine helere.

44. MS euenig   46. treowe: *from margin;* swete: *in text*
47. Thi . . . brouchte: *from margin;* thu bring us in to: *in text*
49. Seolcudliche: *from margin* (d̄ = ð *uncrossed*); Sweteliche: *in text*
52. MS þu sscholdest

50–52. 'That thou . . . shouldest bear in thy bosom the one whom all this world could not encompass'

B

Tho Godes Sune alichte wolde
On eorthe al for ure sake,
Herre teyen he him nolde
Thene that maide to beon his make.   60
Betere ne michte he thaiy he wolde
Ne swetture thing on eorthe take.
Leuedi, bring us to thine bolde
And sschild us from helle wrake.

                                    Amen.

11   *A, Iesu Crist That Ous Is Boue*   Before 1282

Bodl. MS Digby 86, f. 134ᵛ, col. 1. Not in Index. *For date see Brown* XIII, *Introd.,
pp. xxviii ff.*

A, Iesu Crist that ous is boue,
For his swete moder loue
Let ous swetthe werkes werche
And so to serui holi chirche
That we moten ben iborewe   5
And ibrout from alle serewe;
For thilke that beth iborene, iwis,
Hoe wendeth into paradise
To wowe God that we mote
Hounderfongen heueriche bote.   10

12   *Somer Is Comen and Winter Gon*   Mid 13 c. or after

Another instance of secular conventions adapted to religious use, here in a
devotion to Jesus which is also a piece about the Passion: see Poem 15. The turn
from winter to spring is both suitable to Lent and a beginning for the 'I' who
speaks—a captive knight sighing for the 'child' who is to free him. Like the
Christian mood before Easter in contrast with the universal joy, the speaker's
care is widespread in current love song: see Poems 18, 66–69, 71, 121, 135, 136
and their commentaries. The present opening, followed by gradual disclosure
that the questing child is Jesus and the captivity man's worldly life, leads to a

description of the Crucifixion and finally an exhortation, where 'I' thinks to include 'us'.

The poem is thus a kind of metaphoric statement of a Christian's meditation on the Passion. Its power rests in its mixture of romance with realism and caricature (*cf* especially the Jews in stanza 3: 'Ac arst we sullen / Scumi him / a throwe'), in its shift of reader expectation from adventure to the drama of the Passion by the deliberate exploitation of an opening ambiguity, and in its raising of emotion from the circumstances of the 'I', who in the end makes us part of him and the experience immediate to all Christians. For another such deliberate artistic manipulation of the conventions of romance and realism, see *Modern Philology* LVIII (1960–61), pp. 153–73.

BM MS Egerton 613, f. 1ᵛ. Index 3221. Brown XIII, 54.

Somer is comen and winter gon,
This day biginnit to longe,
And this foules euerichon
Ioye hem wit songe.
Son stronge kare me bint   5
Al wit ioye that is funde
In londe,
Al for a child
That is so mild
Of honde.   10

That child that is so milde and wlong
And eke of grete munde,
Bothe in boskes and in bank
Isout me hauet astunde.
Ifunde he heuede me   15
For an appel of a tre
Ibunde.
He brac the bond
That was so strong
Wit wunde.   20

That child that was so milde and wlong
To me alute lowe.
Fram me to Giwes he was sold,

21. MS wilde

Ne cuthen hey him nout cnowe.
'Do we,' sayden he,   25
'Naile we him opon a tre
A lowe,
Ac arst we sullen
Scumi him
A throwe.'   30

Ihesu is the childes name,
King of al londe.
Of the king he meden game
And smiten him wit honde
To fonden him, opon a tre   35
He yeuen him wundes to and thre
Mid honden.
Of bitter drinck
He senden him
A sonde.   40

Det he nom ho rode tre,
The lif of us alle,
Ne miitte it nowtt other be
Bote we scolden walle
And wallen in helle dep   45
Nere neuer so swet
Wit alle.
Ne miitte us saui
Castel, tur
Ne halle.   50

Mayde and moder thar astod,
Marie ful of grace,
And of here eyen heo let blod
Uallen in the place,
The trace ran of here blod.   55

37. MS mi
43. Ne . . . it: MS *erasure; in margin 14c. hand:* ne mytte hit
53. MS *partly illegible by erasure; in margin 14c. hand:* Hii let the teres al of blod

Changed were fles and blod
And face,
He was todrawe
So dur islawe
In chace.   60

Det he nam, the suete man,
Wel heye opon the rode.
He wes hure sunnes euerichon
Mid is swete blode.
Mid flode he lute adun   65
And brace the yates of that prisun
That stode,
And ches here
Out that there
Were gode.   70

He ros him ene the thridde day
And sette him on is trone.
He wule come a domesday
To dem us euerich one.
Grone he may and wepen ay,   75
The man that deiet witoute lay
Alone.
Grante ous, Crist,
Wit thin uprist
To gone.   Amen.   80

13   *Vbi Sount Qui Ante Nos Fuerount*   Before 1282

This homiletic poem belongs with others, English and Continental, variously
abjuring the charms of the present world or regretting their passage: *cf* Poems 8
and especially 47 and their commentaries. Its *de contemptu mundi* emphasis,
intended to stiffen its addressee's opposition to worldliness, makes use of the
widespread figure of the Christian as a knight carrying the Cross for a staff

56. Changed were: MS changedere
74. MS euerichic   **80.** MS gene

and the shield of faith for defence against the Devil. The *Ubi sunt* theme, best known in modern times from Villon's *Where are the Snows of Yesteryear*, goes back to the apocryphal book of Baruch III. 16–19, and is provided with its most famous single medieval examples (on the fading of fame) in Boethius, *De consolatione philosophiae* II, m. vii; but is especially developed in the so-called Sayings of St. Bernard, contemporary with the present poem, and occurs in a variety of contexts, especially the Latin piece *Cur Mundus Militat*: see Brown's Notes, p. 202.

The three opening stanzas suggest poignantly the colour of courtly life in the painted miniatures of the next century, and the gay milieu and bitter sweet of *Sir Gawain and the Green Knight*. See also Poems 10 and 103 and their commentaries.

Oxf. MS Digby 86, f. 126ᵛ–27. Index 3310. Brown XIII, 48.

Were beth they biforen vs weren,
Houndes ladden and hauekes beren
And hadden feld and wode?
The riche leuedies in hoere bour
That wereden gold in hoere tressour   5
With hoere brihtte rode?

Eten and drounken and maden hem glad,
Hoere lif was al with gamen ilad.
Men keneleden hem biforen,
They beren hem wel swithe heye   10
And in a twincling of on eye
Hoere soules weren forloren.

Were is that lawing and that song,
That trayling and that proude yong,
Tho hauekes and tho houndes?   15
Al that ioye is went away,
That wele is comen to weylaway,
To manie harde stoundes.

Hoere paradis hy nomen here
And nou they lien in helle ifere,   20
The fuir hit brennes heuere.

Long is 'ay' and long is 'ho,'
Long is 'wy' and long is 'wo':
Thennes ne cometh they neuere.

Drehy here, man, thenne if thou wilt   25
A luitel pine that me the bit,
Withdrau thine eyses ofte.
They thi pine be ounrede
And thou thenke on thi mede
Hit sal the thinken softe.   30

If that fend, that foule thing,
Thorou wikke roun, thorou fals egging,
There nethere the haueth icast,
Oup and be god champioun!
Stond ne fal namore adoun   35
For a luytel blast.

Thou tak the rode to thi staf
And thenk on him that thereonne yaf
His lif that wes so lef.
He hit yaf for the, thou yelde hit him;   40
Ayein his fo that staf thou nim
And wrek him of that thef.

Of rihtte bileue thou nim that sheld,
The wiles that thou best in that feld
Thin hond to strenkthen fonde.   45
And kep thy fo with staves ord,
And do that traytre seien that word,
Biget that mvrie londe.

Thereinne is day withhouten niht,
Withouten ende strenkthe and miht   50
And wreche of euerich fo,
Mid God Himselwen eche lif
And pes and rest withoute strif,
Wele withouten wo.

Mayden moder, heuene quene,   55
Thou miht and const and owest to bene
Oure sheld ayein the fende.
Help ous sunne for to flen
That we moten thi sone iseen
In ioye withouten hende.   60

Amen.

14   *On Rode Ihesu My Lemman*   13 c.

A brief meditation on the Passion, like Poem 5, but with a wider view of the
Crucifixion scene (lines 3 and 4: 'An besiden him stonden / Marie an Iohan')
and, in this version, a repeated lyric statement at the end (lines 10–12). See
Woolf, pp. 33–4, and for the relation to the Latin *Respice in faciem Christi*,
pp. 30ff and Brown's Notes, p. 194.

BM MS Royal 12 E. 1, f. 194ᵛ. Index 3965. Brown XIII, 35B.

Quanne hic se on rode
Ihesu mi lemman;
An besiden him stonden
Marie an Iohan,
And his rig isuongen   5
And his side istungen
For the luue of man;
Wel ou hic to wepen
And sinnes forleten
Yif hic of luue kan,   10
Yif hic of luue kan,
Yif hic of luue kan.

15   *Nv Yh She Blostme Sprynge*   Later 13 c.

Like Poem 12 this piece adapts love song convention to the Passion but
with differences in technique, emotion and intent. The rapid disclosure that the
beloved is Jesus quickly shifts the reader's expectation, and the 'I', no captive
here and in tune with the spring, does not sigh, but instead sings a glad song

even as he thinks about the Passion. He remains, moreover, at the emotional centre throughout, stands where Mary and John stand (line 21) and prays to be able to serve Jesus, addressing him with the zeal of the lover.

BM MS Royal 2. F. viii, f. 1ᵛ. Index 3963. Brown XIII, 63.

Nv yh she blostme sprynge,
Hic herde a fuheles song,
A swete longinge
Myn herte thurethhut sprong
That is of luue newe   5
That is so swete and trewe
Hyt gladiet al my song.
Hic wot mid ywisse
My lyf an heke my blysse
Is al tharhon ylong.   10

Of Iesu Crist hi synge,
That is so fayr and fre,
Swetest of alle thynge,
Hys owwe hic ohe wel boe.
Wl fer he me sothte,   15
Myd hard he me bothte,
Wyth wnde to and three.
Wel sore he was yswunge
And for me myd spere istunge,
Ynayled to the tree.   20

Wan hic myself stond
And myd herte ysee
Ytherled fetd and onde
Wyt grete neyles three,
Blody was hys eved.   25
Of hym nas novt byleved
Thet of pyne were vre.
Wel othte myn herte

7. MS þong

26-7. 'Those who had not experienced torment did not believe it of him'
B*

Al for hys lvue smerte
Syc and sory be.   30

Away! that hy ne can
To hym tvrne al my thovt
And makien hym my lefman
That thvs me haued hybovt
Wyt pine and sorewhe longe,   35
Wyt wnde depe and stronge.
Of luue ne can hy novt.
Hys blod fel to the grvnde
Hut of ys swete wnde
That of pyne hvs hauet hybrovt.   40

Iesu, lefman suete,
Thv hyef me strenghte and mytht,
Longinge sore and ofte,
To servi the arytht
And lerne pine drye   45
Al for the, swete Marie,
That art so fayr and brytht. . . .

16   *Hi Sike Al Wan Hi Singe*   Later 13 c.

Another love song, like Poem 15, but this time a sigh, whose object is Jesus
and moment the Passion. Technically it is notable as evoking through the
attitudes of the lover the known convention of a spring setting which is never
stated directly in its lines. *Cf* Poem 2 and the last paragraph of its commentary.
Oxf. MS Digby 2, f. 6. Index *1365. Brown* XIII, *64.*

Hi sike al wan hi singe
For sorue that hi se
Wan hic wit wepinge
Biholde apon the tre.
Hi se Ihesu, mi suete,   5

45. And lerne: MS a lene

His herte blode forlete
For the luue of me;
His wondis waxin wete.
Marie, milde and suete,
Thu haf merci of me.   10

Hey apon a dune
As al folke hit se may,
A mile wythute the tune
Abute the midday,
The rode was op areride.   15
His frendis werin al offerde,
Thei clungin so the cley.
The rod stonit in ston,
Marie hirselfe alhon;
Hir songe was 'Wayleway.'   20

Wan hic him biholde
Wyt hey and herte bothe,
Hi se his bodi colde,
His ble waxit alle bloe.
He honge al of blode   25
Se hey apon the rode
Bitwixen thefis two:
Hu soldi singe mor?
Mari, thw wepe sor,
Thu wist of al his woe.   30

Wel ofte wan hi siche
Ande hi make mi mone,
Hiuel hit may me like;
And wondir nis hit non
Wan hi se honge hey   35
Ande bitter peynis drei

9. MS sute   **20.** Wayleway: MS way le
32. Ande hi: MS hi

---

17. 'They shrivelled as the clay does'

Ihesu mi lemmon.
His wondis sor smerte,
The sper his at his herte
Ande thorit his side gon.   40

The naylis beit al to stronge,
The smyt his al to sleye,
Thue bledis al to longe,
The tre his al to heye;
The stonis waxin wete.   45
Allas! Ihesu, mi suete,
Feu frendis hafdis neye
But Sin Ion murnind
And Mari wepind
That al thi sorue seye.   50

Wel ofte wan hi slepe
Wit soru hic ham soht,
Wan hi wake and wende
Hi thenke in mi thoht,
'Allas! that men beit wode: 55
Biholdit an the rode
And silit (hic li notht)
Her souelis into sin
For any worldhis win,
That was so der hibotht.'   60

40. gon: MS on *rubbed and illegible*   41. stronge: MS longe
47. MS ney   48. MS murind
52, 54. MS soit, þoit

Secular Poems of the Thirteenth Century

Untouched by the current poetic use of Nature for love or to sermonize the passing of worldly things, this poem is a pure spring song, or *reverdie*, which voices a general joy at Nature's renewal and whose only 'moral' is that the cuckoo sing and never stop (*cf Carmina Cantabrigiensia* X. ix, to Philomela: *numquam cessa canere*; there are other parallels in that collection and in the *Carmina Burana*). This mood and meaning is imitated by the music and its manner of performance, indications for both of which survive in the MS. For musically the piece, called a *rota*, is an 'infinite canon at the unison of four voices' (Dom A. Hughes, *Early Medieval Music up to 1300* [*New Oxford Hist. Music* II (1954)], pp. 142*ff*), i.e. of voices which successively repeat one another, as some singers begin while others pause and pause as others begin, and so on and on.

The one crux in the text is the meaning of 'uerteth' in line 10, which all current editors gloss as 'breaks wind'. Such joy! But this is a first occurrence in English with that supposed meaning, allegedly from an old English verb '*feortan': see *Middle Engl. Dictionary*, s.v. Ferten, *NED*, s.v. Fart v., 1, and *Early Middle English Verse and Prose* (second edition, Oxford, 1968), glossary. It is tempting, however, in the absence of contrary evidence, to ask whether this is not an early example of 'vert', meaning 'to paw up', or 'to twist' or 'turn', from Latin *vertere*: see *NED*, v., 1 and 2. Ebullience is a virtue but so is poetic relevance. With respect then, may we not suggest

bullock leaps, buck cavorts?

For still another view, see Burney's *General History of Music* II (London, 1782), p. 411, note s.

BM MS Harley 978, f. 11ᵛ. Index 3223. Brown XIII, 6. For date and provenance see, besides Brown's Notes, M. F. Bukofzer, in Univ. Calif. Publ. in Music II (1944), pp. 79ff, and B. Schofield, in Music Review IX (1948), pp. 81ff. For music see especially H. E. Wooldridge, Early English Harmony I (1897), plate 22 (facsimile), and Oxford Hist. Music, edited by Wooldridge (second edition, 1929), I, 85 (transcription) and hear Argo Record RG 443, item 1 (modern performance, with notes on the music and with facsimile in colour on the jacket).

Sing cuccu nu, sing cuccu!
Sing cuccu, sing cuccu nu!

Svmer is icumen in,
Lhude sing cuccu!
Groweth sed and bloweth med   5
And springeth the wde nu,
Sing cuccu!

Awe bleteth after lomb,
Lhouth after calue cu,
Bulluc sterteth, bucke uerteth,   10
Murie sing cuccu!
Cuccu, cuccu,
Wel singes thu cuccu,
Ne swik thu nauer nu!

18   *Mulch Sorw I Walke With*   Earlier 13 c. (?)

   The fretting lover out of tune with Nature is conventional, as is the language
(see the notes beneath the text), but the selection of birds and fishes, woods
and stream—all of them general—to suggest place, moment and mood, is a
notable piece of poetic shorthand. See commentary on Poem 19. See also
introduction, pp. 5 and 6.

Oxf. MS Douce 139, f. 5. Index 864. Brown XIII, 8. For music see Stainer, Early
Bodl. Music *I, plate vi, and II, 10–11 (facsimile and transcription),* Wooldridge,
Early Engl. Harmony *I, plate 7 (facsimile),* Hughes, Early Med. Music, *p. 343
(transcription); and hear Argo Record RG 443, item 2.*

Foweles in the frith,
The fisses in the flod,
And I mon waxe wod:
Mulch sorw I walke with
For beste of bon and blod.   5

18. **4.** MS Multh

18. **5.** *beste . . . blod:* living creature', i.e. a beloved; *cf* below, Poem 68, line 10:
A burde of blod ant of bon; and Poem 33, lines 7–8: *Bestis and thos foules, the fisses
in the flode, /And euch schef aliues imakid of bone and blode*

19   *Ej! Ej! What This Nicht Is Long*   Earlier 13 c.

Another piece whose brevity, like that of Poems 2 and 18, condenses an
emotion which implies a larger circumstance. The time is night, the season
winter, the speaker one who mourns. The convention is the use of *cursus
annorum* and Nature to mirror the speaker's mood, just as convention suggests
that the 'wrong', not otherwise specified, has in fact to do with love. See also
introduction, pp. 5 and 6.

*Oxf. MS Rawlinson G. 22, f. 1ᵛ. Index 2163. Brown XIII, 7. For music see Stainer,
Early Bodl. Music I, plate iii and II, 5 (facsimile and transcription), and hear Argo
Record RG 443, item 5.*

> Mirie it is while sumer ilast
> With fugheles song,
> Oc nu necheth windes blast
> And weder strong.
> Ej! Ej! what this nicht is long,   5
> And ich with wel michel wrong
> Soregh and murne and fast.

20   *Amor Est Quedam Mentis Insania*   Earlier 13 c. (?)

*Oxf. MS Douce 139, f. 157. Index 2005. Brown XIII, 9, and for other definitions
Brown's Notes and Walther, Initia 5579a and 5567.*

> *Amor est quedam mentis insania
> Que vagum hominem ducit per deuia,
> Sitit delicias et bibit tristia,
> Crebris doloribus commiscens gaudia.*
>
> *Amur est une pensee enragee   5
> Ke le vdif humme meyne par veie deueye,
> Ke a soyf de delices e ne beyt ke tristesces
> Ed od souuens dolurs medle sa ioliesces.*

19. **1.** MS Irie, *rubr.* M *missing*   19. **5.** is: *supplied*
19. **6.** MS wid (d = ð *with cross-bar missing*)   19. **7.** fast: *supplied*
20. **8.** ioliesces: MS tristesce

Loue is a selkud wodenesse
That the idel mon ledeth by wildernesse,   10
That thurstes of wilfulscipe and drinket sorwenesse
And with lomful sorwes menget his blithnesse.

21   *Say Me, Viit in the Brom*   Mid 13 c.

The distillation into a brief dialogue with a fortune-teller of a piece of
traditional wisdom, the narrative setting of which is implied here but specified
by BM MS Addit. 11579 in a Latin exemplum embodying these verses. The
advice occurs variously in two Franciscan compilations, the *Gesta Romanorum*
(see Brown's Notes) and the *Fasciculus Morum*, e.g. Oxf. MS Rawl. C670,
f. 10: 'Jacobus 1°. Sit omnis homo velox ad audiendum, tardus ad loquendum.
Vnde bene anglice dicitur:

> Se and here and holde the stylle
> Yefe thou wolte lyue and haue thy wylle.'

Camb. Trinity Coll. MS 323, f. 28. Index *3078.* Brown XIII, *21.*

'Say me, viit in the brom,
Teche me wou I sule don
That min hosebonde
Me louien wolde.'

'Holde thine tunke stille   5
And hawe al thine wille.'

22   *Nou Sprinkes the Sprai*   Late 13/14 c.

Written on the margin of a legal manuscript, this fugitive piece is one of the
earliest recorded carols. It adapts a French original, in which a love-driven
speaker, wandering out in the country to 'play', meets and wins a deserted,
furious maiden: see H. E. Sandison, *The Chanson d'Aventure in Middle English*
(Bryn Mawr Monographs, 1913), pp. 47–8, and Brown's Notes. But the English
piece, which ends abruptly and may be incomplete, only suggests (lines 25–6)
and does not state the French conclusion.

London, Lincoln's Inn MS Hale CXXXV, f. 137ᵛ. Index *360.* Brown XIII, *62.*
Greene *450.*

Nou sprinkes the sprai,
Al for loue icche am so seek
That slepen I ne mai.

Als I me rode this endre dai
O mi pleyinge,   5
Seih icche hwar a litel mai
Bigan to singge,
'The clot him clingge!
Wai bes him i louue longinge
Sal libben ai.   10
          Nou sprinkes, etc.'

Son icche herde that mirie note,
Thider I drogh.
I fonde hire in an herber swote
Under a bogh.   15
With ioie inogh
Son I asked, 'Thou mirie mai,
Hwi sinkestou ai
          Nou sprinkes the sprai, etc.'

Than answerde that maiden swote   20
Midde wordes fewe,
'Mi lemman me haues bihot
Of louue trewe,
He chaunges anewe.
Yiif I mai, it shal him rewe   25
Bi this dai.'
          Now sprinkes, etc.

1. MS *faded, letters between brackets supplied:* [Nou sprinkes th]e
4. MS þis endre dai als i me rode   5. MS *faded, pleyinge:* supplied
6. MS *faded,* icche: *supplied*   8. MS clingges
9. bes . . . longinge: MS es; *where line ends faded,* long[in]ge
13. MS yider   14. MS *faded,* in: *supplied*
25. MS þiif

Religious and Moral Poems
of the Fourteenth Century

23   *Thole a Litel*   Early 14 c.

A moving translation of St Augustine's words in *Confessions* VIII, v, § 12.
Oxford, New Coll. MS F. 88, f. 181ᵛ. Index 1978. Brown XIV, 5.

*Non erat quid responderem tibi . . . , nisi uerba lenta et sompnolenta: 'Modo,
ecce modo, sine paululum.' Sed 'modo et modo' non habebant modum et 'sine
paululum' in longum ibat.*

> Louerd, thu clepedest me
> An ich nagt ne ansuarede the
> Bute wordes scloe and sclepie:
> 'Thole yet, thole a litel.'
> Bute 'yiet and yiet' was endelis   5
> And 'thole a litel' a long wey is.

24   *Popule Meus, Quid Feci Tibi?*   Before 1330
                  By Friar William Herebert

A translation of the Latin *Improperia*, or Good Friday Reproaches, of Christ
against men for the injuries they have done him in return for his sacrifices: see
Gueranger, O. S. B., *The Liturgical Year*, translated by D. L. Shepherd, O. S. B.
(N.Y. 1911), VI, p. 491.
BM MS Addit. 46919, f. 206. Index 2241. Brown XIV, 15.

> My volk, what habbe y do the
> Other in what thyng toened the?
> Gyn nouthe and onswere thou me.

4. MS þet   **5.** MS þiet, þiet

Vor vrom Egypte ich ladde the,
Thou me ledest to rode troe.   5
My volk, what habbe y do the? etc.

Thorou wyldernesse ich ladde the
And uourty yer bihedde the
And aungeles bred ich yaf to the
And into reste ich brouhte the.   10
My volk, what habbe y do the? etc.

What more shulde ich hauen ydon
That thou hauest nouth underuon?
My volk, what habbe y do the? etc.

Ich the vedde and shrudde the,   15
And thou wyth eysyl drinkest to me
And wyth spere styngest me.
My volk, what, etc.

Ich Egypte boeth uor the
And hoere tem y shlou uor the.   20
My volk, what habbe y do the? etc.

Ich delede the see uor the
And pharaon dreynte uor the,
And thou to princes sullest me.
My volk, what habbe y do the? etc.   25

In bem of cloude ich ladde the,
And to Pylate thou ledest me.
My volk, what habbe y do the? etc.

Wyth aungeles mete ich uedde the,
And thou bufetest and scourgest me.   30
My volk, what, etc.

Of the ston ich dronk to the,

3, 23. and: MS ad

And thou wyth galle drincst to me.
My volk, what, etc.

Kynges of Chanaan ich uor the boet,   35
And thou betest my heued wyth roed.
My volk, what, etc.

Ich yaf the croune of kynedom,
And thou me yyfst a croune of thorn.
My volk, what, etc.   40

Ich muchel worshype doede to the,
And thou me hongest on rode troe.
My volk, what, etc.

25   *Aue Maris Stella*   Before 1330
              By Friar William Herebert

A translation of the Latin hymn of the title: Daniel, *Analecta Hymnica* LI
(1908), p. 140, and Dreves, *Anal. Hymn.* II (1888), p. 39.
BM MS Addit. 46919, f. 207ʳᵛ. Index 1054. Brown XIV, 17.

Heyl, leuedy, se stoerre bryht,
Godes moder, edy wyht,
Mayden euer vurst and late,
Of heueneriche sely yate!
Thylk 'aue' that thou vonge in spel   5
Of the aungeles mouth kald Gabriel
In gryht ous sette and shyld vrom shome
That turnst abakward Eues nome.
Gulty monnes bond vnbynd,
Bryng lyht tyl hoem that boeth blynd,   10
Put vrom ous oure sunne
And ern ous alle wynne.
Shou that thou art moder one

8. I.e. Eva, ave

And he vor the take oure bone
That vor ous thy chyld bycom   15
And of the oure kunde nom.
Mayde one thou were myd chylde
Among alle so mylde.
Of sinne ous quite on haste
And make ous meoke and chaste,   20
Lyf thou yyf ous clene,
Wey syker ous yarke and lene
That we Iesus ysoe
And euer blythe boe.

To Uader, Cryst and Holy Gost beo thonk
    and heryinge,   25
To threo persones and o God, o menske
    and worshypinge.

26   *Quis Est Iste Qui Venit de Edom?*   Earlier 14 c.

A paraphrase of *Isaiah* LXIII, 1–7. The *propugnator* of the original, here
rendered 'knight', is regularly taken in this period to be Christ, man's unaided
Champion. See Woolf, pp. 199–202.

BM MS Addit. 46919, f. 208. Index 3906. Brown XIV, 25.

What ys he, thys lordling that cometh vrom the vyht,
Wyth blod-rede wede so grysliche ydyht,
So vayre ycoyntised, so semlich in syht,
So styflyche yongeth, so douhti a knyht?

'Ich hyt am, ich hyt am that ne speke bote ryht,   5
Chaunpyon to helen monkunde in vyht.'

'Why thoenne ys thy schroud red wyth blod al ymeind
Ase troddares in wrynge wyth most al byspreynd?'

'The wrynge ich habbe ytrodded al myself on
And of al monkunde ne was non other won.   10

Ich hoem habbe ytrodded in wrethe and in grome
And al my wede ys byspreynd wyth hoere blod ysome
And al my robe yuuled to hoere grete shome.
The day of thylke wreche leueth in my thouht,
The yer of medes yeldyng ne uoryet ich nouht.   15
Ich loked al aboute some helpynge mon.
Ich souhte al the route bote help nas ther non.
Hyt was myn oune strengthe that thys bote wrouhte,
My owe douhtynesse that help ther me brouhte.
On Godes mylsfolnesse ich wole bythenche me   20
And heryen hym in alle thyng that he yeldeth me.
Ich habbe ytrodded the uolk in wrethe and in grome,
Adreynt al wyth shennesse, ydrawe doun wyth shome.'

27   *Nou Skrnketh Rose ant Lylie Flour*   Before 1340

A poem in praise of the Virgin, combining conventions of secular love with
the homiletic theme of the world's transitoriness. The topic of Mary *physica* is
based ultimately on the widespread metaphor of Christian love and wisdom as
medicines against moral and spiritual disease in the post-lapsarian world (see,
e.g., the 12 c. *Didascalicon* of Hugh of St. Victor and Poem 103 and its com-
mentary), but is also related to the secular theme of love as disease and the lady's
favour as its cure (see Poem 70 and its commentary).

Though the Passion is referred to, it is not the occasion of the present piece;
for the time is summer and the lover walks out to 'play' as in a French *chanson
d'aventure*, its Gallic particularity made English by local reference: see Poem 22
and its commentary. In one aspect, therefore, the piece is like the lover's praise
of a secular lady, adverting to the usual theme of variance and invariance (see
Poems 118, 119 and 140); in another it is a moral poem on the general topic of
worldly impermanence. The opening verses, fragrant with summer flowers,
are suitable to worldly *amour* yet belong with that seasonal poetry, ancient in
time and European in range, whose subject is the *cursus annorum*, whose moral
is the swift passage from life to death, and whose emotion is the poignant regret
for the loveliness that fades: see Poems 13, 30, and especially 47 and their
commentaries. Both worlds of love, secular and moral-religious, are touched by
the Platonic contrast between the fleshly and the ideal, the fleeting and the
permanent, as found, e.g., in Apuleius, *De Platone*, and that 'bible' of secular
love, Andreas Capellanus, *De Arte Honesti Amandi*, both influential in this
period.

The power of the present poem thus resides in a double transformation by
secular *chanson* of Marian eulogy and *Ubi sunt*, in which the conventions of all
three mingle 'naturally' and the mood moves from disenchanted discovery to
zeal, as lover turns from play, not as in Poem 22 to another 'play', but to a new
and more permanent devotion.

*BM MS Harley 2253, f. 80, col. 2. Index 2359. Brown XIV, 10. Brook 23. EETS,
o.s. 225 (1965), with introduction by N. R. Ker (facsimile). For date see Brown's
introduction, p. xiii.*

Nou skrnketh rose ant lylie flour
That whilen ber that suete sauour
In somer that suete tyde,
Ne is no quene so stark ne stour
Ne no leuedy so bryht in bour   5
That ded ne shal byglyde.
Whose wol fleysh lust forgon
Ant heuene blis abyde,
On Ihesu be is thoht anon
That therled was ys side.   10

From Petresbourh in o morewenyng
As y me wende o my pleyyyng
On mi folie y thohte;
Menen y gon my mournyng
To hire that ber the heuene kyng,   15
Of merci hire bysohte:
'Ledy, preye thi sone for ous.
That vs duere bohte,
Ant shild vs from the lothe hous
That to the Fend is wrohte.'   20

Myn herte of dedes wes fordred
Of synne that y haue my fleish fed
Ant folewed al my tyme,
That y not whider I shal be led
When y lygge on dethes bed   25
In ioie ore into pyne.
On o ledy myn hope is,

Moder ant virgyne,
Whe shulen into heuene blis
Thurh hire medicine.   30

Betere is hire medycyn
Then eny mede or eny wyn,
Hire erbes smulleth suete;
From Catenas into Dyuelyn
Nis ther no leche so fyn   35
Oure serewes to bete.
Mon that feleth eni sor
Ant his folie wol lete,
Withoute gold other eny tresor
He mai be sound ant sete.   40

Of penaunce is his plastre al
Ant euer seruen hire y shal
Nou ant al my lyue.
Nou is fre that er was thral
Al thourh that leuedy gent ant smal: 45
Heried be hyr ioies fyue.
Wherso eny sek ys
Thider hye blyue.
Thurh hire beoth ybroht to blis
Bo mayde ant wyue.   50

For he that dude is body on tre
Of oure sunnes haue piete
That weldes heouene boures.
Wymmon, with thi iolyfte
Thou thench on Godes shoures.   55
Thah thou be whyt ant bryth on ble,
Falewen shule thy floures.
Iesu, haue merci of me,
That al this world honoures.
                              Amen.

55, 56. *transposed in* MS   58. me. MS vs

28   *Mayden Moder Milde, Me Menez*   Before 1340
                              de Tresoun

A macaronic piece which like Poem 10 is both praise of the Virgin and
supplication, this time by a prisoner in the toils who uses the figure, among
others, of the shield against the Devil.

BM MS Harley 2253, f. 83. Index 2039. Brown XIII, 87. Brook 28. EETS, o.s. 255
(*facsimile*).

> Mayden moder milde,
> Oiez cel oreysoun:
> From shome thou me shilde
> E de ly mal feloun.
> For love of thine childe   5
> Me menez de tresoun;
> Ich wes wod ant wilde,
> Ore su en prisoun.
>
> Thou art feyr ant fre
> E plein de doucour;   10
> Of the sprong the ble,
> Ly souerein creatour.
> Mayde, byseche y the
> Vostre seint socour;
> Meoke ant mylde, be with me   15
> Pur la sue amour.
>
> Tho Iudas Iesum founde
> Donque ly beysa,
> He wes bete ant bounde
> Que nus tous fourma   20
> Wyde were is wounde
> Qe le Gyw ly dona;

2. 'Hear this prayer'   **4.** 'And from the evil felon', i.e. the Devil
6. 'Take me away from (his) treachery'   **8.** 'Now I am in prison'
10. 'And full of sweetness'   **14.** 'Your blessed aid'
16. 'For love of him'   **18.** 'Then kissed him'
20. 'He who formed us all'   **22.** 'Which the Jews gave him'

He tholede harde stounde,
Me poi le greua.

On stou ase thou stode,   25
Pucele, tot pensaunt,
Thou restest the vnder rode,
Ton fitz veites pendant.
Thou seye is sides of blode,
L'alme de ly partaunt;   30
He ferede vch an fode
En mound que fust viuaunt.

Ys siden were sore,
Le sang de ly cora;
That lond wes forlore,   35
Mais il le rechata.
Vch bern that wes ybore
En enfern descenda;
He tholede deth therfore,
En ciel puis mounta.   40

Tho Pilat herde the tydynge
Molt fu ioyous baroun;
He lette byfore him brynge
Iesu Nazaroun.
He was ycrouned kynge   45
Pur nostre redempcioun.
Whose wol me synge
Auera grant pardoun.

24. 'I am too little grieved for it'   26. 'Maiden, lost in thought'
28. 'You see your Son hanging'   30. 'The soul parting from him'
32. 'Who lived in the world'   34. 'The blood ran from them'
36. 'But he redeemed it'   38. 'Descended into Hell'
40. 'Then mounted into Heaven'   42. 'He was a very joyous lord'
46. 'For our redemption'   48. 'Will get great pardon'

Hou Loue Hym Haueth Ybounde

This poem, also employing the Passion for the amatory theme, is followed
in the MS by Poem 71, and both together, in like verse patterns and parallel
phrases, deal with the contrast between religious and secular love. Despite the
lyric refrain, however, didactic contrast tends to supervene upon emotion and
even when read separately each piece plays with the substance of a definition.
For the question of whether the present piece represents a pious rewriting of
its secular counterpart, see Brown's and Brook's Notes.

BM MS Harley, 2253, f. 128. Index *1922. Brown XIII, 90. Brook 31. EETS, o.s.
255 (facsimile).*

Lvtel wot hit any mon
Hou loue hym haueth ybounde
That for vs o the rode ron
Ant bohte vs with is wounde.
The loue of him vs haueth ymaked sounde   5
Ant ycast the grimly gost to grounde.
Euer ant oo, nyht ant day, he haueth vs in is thohte;
He nul nout leose that he so deore bohte.

He bohte vs with is holy blod,
What shulde he don vs more?   10
He is so meoke, milde ant good,
He na gulte nout therfore.
That we han ydon y rede we reowen sore
Ant crien euer to Iesu, 'Crist, thyn ore!'
Euer ant oo, niht ant day, etc.   15

He seh his fader so wonder wroht
With mon that wes yfalle,
With herte sor he seide is oht
Whe shulde abuggen all.
His suete sone to hym gon clepe ant calle   20
Ant preiede he moste deye for vs alle.
Euer ant oo, etc.

He brohte vs alle from the deth
Ant dude vs frendes dede.

Suete Iesu of Nazareth,   25
Thou do vs heuene mede.
Vpon the rode why nulle we taken hede?
His grene wounde so grimly conne blede.
Euer ant oo, etc.

His deope wounden bledeth fast,   30
Of hem we ohte munne.
He hath ous out of helle ycast,
Ybroht vs out of sunne.
For loue of vs his wonges waxeth thunne;
His herte blod he yef for al monkunne.   35
Euer ant oo, etc.

30   *Wynter Wakeneth Al My Care*   Before 1340

A brief song on the theme of transitoriness, with the winter opening and its
bare leaves used to introduce a meditation on the end of all things in death and
an attempt to find stability amidst instability by an appeal to Jesus. For the
language, topics and association of the cycle of Nature with this theme, see
Poems 47 and 27 and their commentaries, and contrast the development of
Poem 19; also *cf* line 15 with Poem 6 and Poems 33, lines 15–16, and 46,
lines 22–4, 33–6.

*BM MS Harley 2253, f. 75ᵛ, col. 2. Index 4177. Brown XIV, 9. Brook 17. EETS,
o.s. 255 (facsimile).*

Wynter wakeneth al my care,
Nou this leues waxeth bare;
Ofte y sike ant mourne sare
When hit cometh in my thoht
Of this worldes ioie hou hit geth al to noht.   5

Nou hit is ant nou hit nys
Also hit ner nere ywys.
That moni mon seith, soth hit ys:
'Al goth bote Godes wille,
Alle we shule deye that vs like ylle.'   10

10. MS þaþ

Al that grein me graueth grene
Nou hit faleweth al bydene.
Ihesu, help that hit be sene
Ant shild vs from helle,
For y not whider y shal ne hou longe her duelle.   15

31   *Wyth What Mastrie*   Mid 14 c.

Oxf. MS Bodley 26, f. 193ᵛ. Index 4207 (cf Supplement 2231.8).

Wyth what mastrie
He hat man ywrouht,
Wyth what curtaysie
He ys to man ybrouht,
Wyth what marchandie   5
He hat ybouht
And what seynorie
He hat to man ythouht.

32   *My Dohther, My Derlyng*   Mid 14 c.

Man's brief history moralized and turned to carol form, with a Latin version
in which the line *audi filia et vide* parallels the two-line English burden.
Oxf. MS Bodley 26, f. 193ᵛ. Supplement 2231.8. Robbins, in MLN LIII, 243.

    Audi ergo et vide
Principium a quo processisti,
Priuilegium quale suscepisti,
Preiudicium quantum commisisti,
Precipicium in quod incidisti.   5

    My dohter, my derlyng,
    Herkne my lore, yse my techyng:

11. grein: MS gren

How mankende furst bygan,
In what manschepe now ys man,
What wykedness man hat ydo,   10
What ioye and blisse man ys ybroht.
    My dohter, my derlyng,
    Herkne my lore, yse my thechyng.

33   *Lollai, Litil Child, Whi Wepistou?*   Mid 14c. or before

A homiletic piece on transiency and man's intransigence, made moving by
incorporation in a secular lullaby. The sermonizing themes are commonplace
(man's source and end, fickle Fortune, life as pilgrimage) and some of the
language echoes other poems (*cf*, e.g., lines 7–9 with Poem 18, line 5; lines 19–22
with Poem 38; and lines 15–16 with Poem 6 and Poems 30, line 15, and 46,
lines 22–4 and 33–6); but the negative *contemptus mundi* nuance is controlled by
a particular occasion—mother hushing child and meditating sadly on the
sorrow it will feel in a world where only man does himself no good.

BM MS Harley 913, f. 32ʳᵛ. Index 2025. Brown XIV 28. For the Latin, Walther,
Initia 10380. The Latin version, probably made from the English, occurs in the same
MS on f. 63ᵛ.

Lollai, lollai, litil child, whi wepistou so sore?
Nedis mostou wepe, hit was iyarkid the yore
Euer to lib in sorow, and sich and mourne therefore
As thin eldren did er this while hi aliues wore.
Lollai, lollai, litil child, child lolai, lullow.   5
Into vncuth world incommen so ertow.

Bestis and thos foules, the fisses in the flode,
And euch schef aliues imakid of bone and blode,
Whan hi commith to the world hi doth ham silf sum gode;
Al bot the wrech brol that is of Adamis blode.   10
Lollai, lollai, litil child, to kar ertou bemette;
Thou nost noht this worldis wild befor the is isette.

3. therefore: MS euer; cf *Brown XIV, 28, Note to stanza 1*
4. wore: MS were; cf *Brown, ibid.*   **5.** Lollai, lollai: MS lollai

7–8. Cf. Poem 18, lines 1, 2 and 5, and Poem 68, line 10

Child, if betidith that thou ssalt thriue and the,
Thench thou were ifostred vp thi moder kne.
Euer hab mund in thi hert of thos thinges three: 15
When thou commist, wham thou art and what ssal com
    of the.
Lollai, lollai, litil child, child lollai, lollai,
With sorow thou com into this world, with sorow ssalt
    wend awai.

Ne tristou to this world, hit is thi ful vo,
The rich he makith pouer, the pore rich also;   20
Hit turneth wo to wel and ek wel to wo.
Ne trist no man to this world, whil hit turnith so.
Lollai, lollai, litil child, thi fote is in the whele.
Thou nost whoder turne to wo other wele.

Child, thou ert a pilgrim in wikidnis ibor,   25
Thou wandrest in this fals world, thou loke the bifor.
Deth ssal com with a blast vt of a well dim horre
Adamis kin dun to cast, him silf hath ido befor.
Lollai, lollai, litil child, so wo the wroth Adam
In the lond of paradise throh wikidnes of Satan.   30

Child, thou nert a pilgrim bot an vncuthe gist,
Thi dawes beth itold, thi iurneis beth icast,
Whoder thou salt wend north or est
Deth the sal betide with bitter bale in brest.
Lollai, lollai, litil child, this wo Adam the wroht   35
What he of the appil ete and Eue hit him betacht.

Lolla, lolla, paruule, cur fles tam amare?
Oportet te plangere necnon suspirare,
Te dolere grauiter decet, uegetare
Vt parentes exules nexerant ignare.
Lolla, lolla, paruule, natus mundo tristi,
Ignotum cum maximo dolore uenisti.

23. thi: MS the   1, 11, 17, 23, 29. Lollai, lollai: MS lollai l
29. MS worþ   35. MS lolla l litil chil

Alites et bestie, pisces fluctuantes,
Creature genite, cuncte uegetantes
Sibi prosunt aliqui uiuamen prestantes
Nisi tu, miserime, uiuens inter santes.
Lolla, lolla, paruule, repletus dolore.

34   *O Homo, Vide Quid Pro Te Pacior*   Mid 14c. or before

A version of a Latin poem by Phillip, Chancellor of the University of Paris.
See Poem 54 and its commentary.

BM MS Harley 913, f. 28ᵛ. Index 2047. For Latin, Walther, Initia 8401.

Man, bihold what ic for the
Tholid up the rode tre.
Ne mai no kinnes wo be more
Than min was tho ic heng thare.
Hire me, man, to the gridind,   5
For loue of the biter deiend.
Loke mi pinis biter and strang
Wan ic was nailed thorh fot and hond.
For the ic ad hard stundes,
Dintes grete and sore wondes.   10
For the biter drink ic dronk,
And thou cunnest me no thonk.
Withvte ic was ipined sore,
Within ic was mochil more;
For thou nelt thonk me   15
The loue that ich schowid the.

35   *Aurora Lucis Rutilat*   Mid 14 c.

A translation of the first two stanzas of an Easter hymn *ad matutinos Paschae*
(Mone I, 190), in which the rendering '*vs* wreches' (line 8) for Latin *miseros*
implies that the English poem is conceived as the speech of one of the Patriarchs
or Prophets released from Hell by Christ at its Harrowing.

Oxf. Merton Coll. MS 248, f. 141ᵛ. Index 2684. Brown XIV, 37.

An ernemorwe the dayliht spryngeth,
The angles in heuene murye syngeth,
The world is blithe and ek glad,
The uendus of helle beth sorwel and mad,
Whanne the kyng, godus sone,   5
The strengthe of the deth hadde ouercome.
Helle dore he brak with his fot
And out of pyne vs wreches he tok.

36   *O Gloriosa Domina Excelsa*   Mid 14 c.

A translation of the last half of a hymn ascribed to Venantius Fortunatus,
which frequently appeared separately in Latin: Mone II, 129–30 (*cf* 128).
*Oxf. Merton Coll. MS 248, f. 148*ᵛ*. Index 1832. Brown* XIV, *38.*

Lefdy blisful, of muchel miht,
Heyere thanne the sterres liht,
Hym the the made wuman best
Thow youe hym souken of thi brest.
Thet thet Eue vs hadde bynome   5
Thow has iyolde thorw thy sone.
Thow art in heuene an hole imad
Thorw which the senful thorwgeth glad.
Thow art the kynges yate idyht,
Brihtore thow art than eny liht.   10
Lif thorw Marye vs is iwrouht,
Alle ben glade thet Crist hath ibouht.

37   *Crux Fidelis*   Mid 14 c.

A translation from the hymn *Pange Lingua Gloriosi* by Venantius Fortunatus
of stanza 8, which was sung separately in the Good Friday service and sometimes
inserted as a refrain between stanzas of the entire hymn: see Mone, I, 131.
Oxf. Merton Coll. MS 248, f. 167. Index 3212. Brown XIV, *40.*

35. **1.** the: MS de

C

Crux fidelis, inter omnes arbor una nobilis,
Nulla silva talem profert fronde, flore, germine.
Dulce lignum dulces clavos, dulce pondus sustinet.

Steddefast crosse, inmong alle other
Thow art a tre mykel of prise.   5
In brawnche and flore swylk another
I ne wot non in wode no rys.
Swete be the nalys
And swete be the tre
And sweter be the birdyn that hangis vppon the.

38   *The Lade Dame Fortune*   Mid 14 c.

Found separately in a number of MSS and incorporated whole in Poem 33,
lines 19–22, these lines as given here are from the 14 c. Franciscan *Fasciculus
Morum*, but in 15 c. copies: see commentary to Poem 51. Brown's Cambridge
text is written on a roll of *c.* 1325 but not necessarily at the same time. There is
also a French version in Ghent U. MS 317.

Oxf. MS Rawlinson C670, f. 72. Index 3408. Brown XIV, 42.

Non est ergo dolendum de amissione temporalium fortuitorum.

The Lade Dame Fortune is bothe frende and foo:
Of pore hee maketh riche and ryche of pore also;
Hee turneth woo to wele and wele also to woo.
Ne trist noght to hir word, the whele turneth so.

39   *Al It Is Fantam*   Mid 14 c.

Camb. Univ. MS Ee. 1. 5, f. 2*ᵛ. Index 190. Brown XIV, 43.

Al it is fantam that we mid fare,
Naked and poure henne we shul fare,
Al shal ben other mannes that we fore care,
But that we don for Godes loue haue we no mare.

38. 4. hir: MS his

40   *De Mundo*   14 C.

This macaronic poem is one of a group of homiletic pieces on the evils of
the time, which include lines on falseness and covetousness: see Brown's texts
and Notes.

Oxf. Merton Coll. MS 248, f. 166. Index *2787. Brown XIV, 39. Walther,*
Sprichwörter *10758.*

> Lex lyis done ofuer al
> Quia fallax fallit vbique
> And loue es bot small
> Quia gens se gestat inique.
>
> Heu, pleps conqueritur   5
> Quod rara fides reperitur.
> Lex iuris moritur,
> Fraus vincit, amor sepelitur.
>
> Hallas, men planys of litel trwthe,
> Hit ys dede and tat is rwthe.   10
> Falsedam regnis and es abowe
> And byrid es trwloue.

41   *Als I Lay Vpon a Nith*   Before 1372

Another poem combining the religious and the secular, on this occasion to
expound a point of doctrine, the Virgin Birth. The *donnée* is the Nativity.
Chanson d'aventure and lover's nocturnal vision join with Marian eulogy to
raise the question of beauty's relation to goodness, and provide the cogent
answer from the lips of the male closest to a woman, her husband. No hint
occurs here, regarding St. Joseph, (see Woolf, p. 150 and *n.* 3) of the *fabliau*
smirk at young wife deceiving ancient spouse—nor could it, and the issue is
settled gently but firmly.

A further piece on the Nativity in the same MS—Brown *XIV,* 56—using
like conventions, is in form quite different. It does not furnish proof of a parti-
cular doctrine but a summary of the coming career of Jesus. The *chanson*-dream

8. MS farus

thus leads to lullaby and dialogue between Mother and Child, and Joseph has no place in it.

Both pieces occur in the Commonplace Book of John Grimestone, written down in 1372.

Nat. Lib. Scotland MS Advocates 18.7.21, ff. 5ᵛ–6. Index 353. Brown XIV, 58. For music, Stainer I, plates lxvii and lxviii (facsimile), and II, 130–31 (transcription)

Als I lay vpon a nith
I lokede vpon a stronde;
I beheld a mayden brith,
A child sche hadde in honde.

Hire loking was so loueli,   5
Hire semblant was so suete,
Of al my sorwe sikerli
Sche mithte my bales bete.

I wondrede of that suete with
An to my self I sayde   10
Sche hadde don makindde vnrith
But yif sche were a mayde.

Be hire sat a sergant
That sadli seide his sawe.
He sempte be is semblant   15
A man of the elde lawe.

His her was hor on heuede,
His ble began to glide,
He herde wel wat I seyde
An bad me faire abide.   20

'Thou wondrest,' he seyde skilfuli,
'On thing thou hast beholde,
And I dede so treuli
Til tales weren me tolde,

16. 'A man of the Old Testament', i.e. a Jew

'Hou a womman sulde ben than   25
Moder an maiden thore,
An withouten wem of man
The child sulde ben bore.

'Althou I vnworthi be,
Sche is Marie, my wif.   30
God wot sche hadde neuere child be me.
I loue hire as my lif.

'But or euere wiste I
Hire wombe began to rise;
I telle the treuthe treuli   35
I not neuere in wat wyse.

'I troste to hire goodnesse,
Sche wolde no thing misdo;
I wot et wel iwisse,
For I haue founded et so   40

'That rathere a maiden sulde
Withouten man conceyue
Than Marie misdon wolde
An so Ioseph deceyue.

'The child that lith so poreli   45
In cloutes al bewent
An bounden so misesli,
Fro heuene he is isent.

'His fader is king of heuene,
An so seide Gabriel,   50
To wam that child is euene,
O Emanuel.'

But this child that I sau than,
And as Ioseph seyde,

36. I not: MS In wot

I wot the child is god an man   55
An is moder mayde.

I thankid him of his lore
With al myn herte mith
That this sith i sau thore
Als I lay on a nyth.   60

This child thanne worchipe we
Bothe day an nith,
That we moun his face se
In ioyye that is so lith.

                     Amen.

42   *Luueli Ter of Loueli Eyye*   Before 1372

A meditation on the Passion by a sorrowing 'I', who perceives what all
meditators recognize. In shape the poem is a carol; its burden, the loveliest
that survives, alternating group refrain with meditator's song, distils yet gentles
emotion by narrowing its attention to Christ's tear.

From the Commonplace Book of John Grimestone, the Franciscan friar. The
book is a collection of sermon materials and notes, and lyrics.

*Nat. Lib. Scotland MS Advocates 18.7.21, f. 124ᵛ. Index 3691. Brown XIV, 69.
Greene 271.*

        Luueli ter of loueli eyye, qui dostu me so wo?
        Sorful ter of sorful eyye, thou brekst myn herte ato.

        Thou sikest sore,
        Thi sorwe is more
        Than mannis muth may telle.   5
        Thou singest of sorwe
        Manken to borwe
        Out of the pit of helle.
        Luueli, etc.

        I proud an kene,   10
        Thou meke an clene

Withouten wo or wile;
Thou art ded for me
An I liue thoru the,
So blissed be that wile.   15
Luueli, etc.

Thi moder seet
Hou wo the beet
An therfore yerne sche yerte.
To hire thou speke   20
Hire sorwe to sleke:
Suet sute wan thin herte.
Luueli, etc.

Thin herte is rent,
Thi bodi is bent   25
Vpon the rode tre.
The weder is went,
The devel is schent,
Crist, thoru the mith of the.
Luueli, etc.   30

43   *I Wolde Ben Clad in Cristes Skyn*   Before 1372

A devotional poem arising from a meditation on the Passion. The figure of
abandoning kith and kin goes back to the Gospels; to escape the world by
merging with the body of Christ is the mystic's most regular yearning, and to
do so by hiding in Christ's wounded side a subject of hymnology: see Mone I,
166, *Ad Latus Domini,* and Daniel II, 371.

From the Commonplace Book of John Grimestone.

Nat. Lib. Scotland MS Advocates 18.7.21, f. 124ᵛ, col. 2. Index *1002. Brown*
XIV, *71.*

Gold an al this werdis wyn
Is nouth but Cristis rode;
I wolde ben clad in Cristes skyn

19. MS yepte   **22.** MS Suet suet

That ran so longe on blode
An gon t'is herte an taken myn in: 5
Ther is a fulsum fode.
Than yef I litel of kith or kyn,
For ther is alle gode.

                              Amen.

44   *O Vos Omnes Qui Transitis per Viam*   Before 1372

One of a number of poems, English and Latin, in which the Crucifixion
image has by implication become a wayside shrine or even a gravestone, its
inscription Christ's words bidding men pause for meditation. The words them-
selves are based on *Lamentations* I. 12, part of which provides the present Latin
title, and belong with the *Improperia*, or Reproaches of Christ, on Good Friday.
See also Poem 55 and Brown *XIV*, 46.

    From Grimestone's Commonplace Book.

Nat. Lib. Scotland MS Advocates 18.7.21, f. 125ᵛ, col. 2. Index 4263. Brown
XIV, *74.*

                Ye that pasen be the weyye,
                Abidet a litel stounde.
                Beholdet, al mi felawes,
                Yef ani me lik is founde.
                To the tre with nailes thre   5
                Wol fast I hange bounde,
                With a spere al thorou mi side
                To min herte is mad a wounde.

45   *My Trewest Tresowre Sa*   Mid 14 c. or after
                    Trayturly Was Taken
                    School of Richard Rolle

Another meditation on the Passion, at whose climax is the sunset and the
figure of Christ the knight with his shield. An example of the highly mannered
alliterative verse of its period, this poem is heavy with metaphors of endear-
ment, and a vocabulary whose choice is affected by *annominatio*.

Camb. Univ. MS Dd. 5. 64, III, ff. 34ᵛ–35. Index 2273. Brown XIV, *79.*

My trewest tresowre sa trayturly was taken,
Sa bytterly bondyn wyth bytand bandes,
How sone of thi seruandes was thou forsaken
And lathly for my lufe hurled with thair handes.

My well of my wele sa wrangwysly wryed,   5
Sa pulled owt of preson to Pilate at prime,
Thaire dulles and thaire dyntes ful drerely thou dreed
Whan thai schot in thi syght bath slauer and slyme.

My hope of my hele say hyed to be hanged,
Sa charged with thi crosce and corond with thorne,   10
Ful sare to thi hert thi steppes tha stanged;
Me thynk thi bak burd breke, it bendes forborne.

My salue of my sare sa saryful in syght,
Sa naked and nayled thi ryg on the rode,
Ful hydusly hyngand, thay heued the on hyght,   15
Thai lete the stab in the stane all stekked that thar stode.

My dereworthly derlyng sa dolefully dyght,
Sa straytly vpryght streyned on the rode,
For thi mykel mekenes, thi mercy, thi myght,
Thow bete al my bales with bote of thi blode.   20

My fender of fose, so fonden in the felde,
Sa lufly lyghtand at the euensang tyde,
Thi moder and hir menyhe vnlaced thi scheld.
Al weped that thar were, thi woundes was sa wyde.

My pereles prynce als pure I the pray,   25
The mynde of this myrour thou lat me noght mysse,
Bot wynd vp my wyle to won wyth the ay
That thou be beryd in my brest and bryng me to blysse.

Amen.

46   *When Adam Delf and Eue Span*   Mid 14 c. or after
                        School of Richard Rolle

Another monitory poem *de contemptu mundi*, made light by smooth verse,
regular rhyme and refrain, and 'popular' by well worn language and themes:
cf, e.g., lines 1–4 with other 'When Adam delf' verses; lines 10–12 with *Wisdom
of Solomon* v. 11 and its uses; lines 22–4 and especially 33–6 with Poem 6 and
Poems 30, line 15 and 33, lines 15–16; and lines 61*ff* with Poem 56. Note also
the statement of the traditional Judgment scene, lines 49–60, in contemporary
courtroom language (see paraphrase of lines 59–60 beneath the text of the poem).
Camb. Univ. MS Dd. 5. 64, III, ff. 35ᵛ–36. Index *3921. Brown* XIV, *81.*

> When Adam delf and Eue span,
> Spir, if thou wil spede,
> Whare was than the pride of man
> That now merres his mede?
> Of erth and slame als was Adam   5
> Maked to noyes and nede
> Are we als he maked to be
> Whil we this lyf sal lede.
> With I and E, born are we,
> Als Salomon vs hyght,   10
> To trauel here whils we ar fere
> Als fouls to the flight.
>
>
> In worlde we ware kast for to kare
> To we be broght to wende
> Til wele or wa, an of tha twa,   15
> To won withouten ende.
> Forthi whils thou may helpe the now
> Amend the and haf mynde,
> When thou sal ga he bese thi fa
> That are was here thi frende.   20
> With E and I, I rede forthi
> Thou thynk apon thies thre:
> What we ar and what we ware
> And what we sal be.

War thou als wyse praysed in pryce   25
Als was Salomon,
Fayrer fode of bone and blode
Then was Absalon,
Strengthy and strang to wreke thi wrang
Als euer was Sampson,   30
Thou ne myght a day, na mare then thai,
Dede withstand allon.
With I and E, dede to the
Sal com, als I the kenne;
Thou ne wate in what state,   35
How ne whare ne when.

Of erth aght that the was raght
Thou sal not haue, I hete,
Bot seuen fote therin to rot
And thi wyndyngschete.   40
Forthi gyf whils thou may lif
Or all gase that thou gete:
Thi gast fra God, thi godes olod,
Thi flesch fowled vndur fete.
With I and E, syker thow be   45
That thi secutowrs
Of the ne wil rek bot skelk and skek
Ful boldly in thi bowrs.

Of welth and witt this sal be hitt
In world that thou here wroght.   50
Rekken thou mon and yelde reson
Of thyng that thou here thoght.
May no falas help in this case
Ne cownsel getes thou noght;
Gyft ne grace nane thare gase   55
Bot brok als thou hase boght.
With I and E, the boke biddes the,
Man, be ware of thi werkes;

53. MS fals

Terme of the yere hase thou nan here,
Thi mede bese ther thi merkes.   60

What may this be that I here se,
The fayrehede of thi face,
Thi ble sa bryght, thi mayn, thi myght,
Thi mowth that miri mas?
Al mon als was to powder passe   65
To dede when thow gase.
A grysely geste bese than thi breste
In armes til enbrase.
With I and E, syker thou be,
Thare es nane, I the hete,   70
Of al thi kyth wald slepe the with
A nyght vnder schete.

47   *Sum Tyme Thenk on Yusterday*   Mid 14 c. or after

One of the most poignant Middle English poems on the theme of transiency,
at the beginning of which, in a genre picture of contemporary society, the
fading present's tempo is increased from the movement of the seasons to the
hurry of a single day. As it develops the poem takes on 'philosophic' breadth,
touching the age-old themes of Shadow and Substance, Age and Youth, the
insensate faithfulness of Death, whose literary traditions, going back to Horace
('pallida mors'), were renewed in many a *poema de morte* by the contemporary
devastation of the Black Plague. The last stanza, coming back full circle to
the opening scene, is a picture from a *Totentanz*. See 'The Art of Sir Gawain
and the Green Knight', *Univ. Toronto Quarterly* XXXIII, especially pp. 263–4;
and *cf* Poems 13, 17 and 20.

*Bodley MS Eng. Poet. a. 1 (Vernon MS), f. 408, col. 1–408ᵛ. Index 3996. Brown
XIV, 101.*

Whon men beoth muriest at heor mele
With mete and drink to maken hem glade,
With worship and with worldlich wele,

2, 3. *Initial* W *supplied.*

59–60. 'You will get here no set delay as granted on earth to a debtor for the
payment of his debts (i.e., justice is immediate), and what is meted out to you
will be what your X's (*merkes*, i.e., your deeds on earth) have established as your
legal obligation.'

Thei ben so set they conne not sade;
Thei haue no deynte for to dele   5
With thinges that ben deuoutli made;
Thei weene heor honour and heore hele
Schal euer laste and neuer diffade.
Bot in heor hertes I wolde thei hade,
Whon thei gon ricchest men on aray,   10
Hou sone that God hem may degrade
And sum tyme thenk on yusterday.

This day as leef we may be liht,
With al the murthes that men may vise,
To reuele with this buirdes briht,   15
Vche mon gayest on his gyse;
At the last hit draweth to niht,
That slep most make his maystrise.
Whon that he hath ikud his miht,
The morwc he bosketh vp to rise,   20
Then al draweth hem to fantasyse.
Wher he is bicomen, con no mon say
(And yif heo wuste thei weore ful wise),
For al is torned to yesterday.

Whose wolde thenke vppon this   25
Mihte fynde a good enchesun whi,
To preue this world, alwei iwis
Hit nis but fantum and feiri.
This erthly ioye, this worldly blis
Is but a fikel fantasy,   30
For nou hit is and now hit nis,
Ther may no mon therinne affy;
Hit chaungeth so ofte and so sodeynly,
Today is her, tomorwe away.
A siker ground ho wol him gy,   35
I rede he thenke on yusterday. . . .

The lyf that eny mon schal lede

21. MS fantasye

Beth certeyn dayes atte last;
Then moste vr terme schorte nede,
Be o day comen, another is past.   40
Herof and we wolde take good hede
And in vr hertes acountes cast,
Day bi day withouten drede
Toward vr ende we draweth ful fast;
Then schal vr bodies in erthe be thrast,   45
Vr careyns chouched vnder clay.
Herof we ouhte beo sore agast
And we wolde thenke on yusterday. . . .

But yit me merueyles ouer al
That God let mony mon croke and elde   50
Whon miht and strengthe is from hem fal
That thei may not hemself awelde;
And now this beggers most principal,
That good ne profyt may non yelde.
To this purpose onswere I schal   55
Whi God sent such men boote and belde:
Crist, that made bothe flour and felde,
Let suche men lyue, forsothe to say,
Whon a yong mon on hem bihelde,
Scholde seo the schap of yesterday. . . .   60

I have wist sin I cuth meen
That children hath bi candel liht
Heor schadewe on the wal isen
And ronne therafter al the niht.
Bisy aboute thei han ben   65
To cacchen hit with al heore miht,
And whon thei cacchen hit best wolde wene,
Sannest hit schet out of heor siht.
The schadewe cacchen thei ne miht
For no lynes that thei couthe lay.   70
This schadewe I may likne ariht
To this world and yusterday. . . .

70. A figure from bird snaring

Wel thou wost withouten fayle
That deth hath manest the to dye,
But whon that he wol the asayle,   75
That wost thou not ne neuer may spye.
Yif thou wolt don be my consayle,
With siker defence beo ay redye,
For siker defence in this batayle
Is clene lyf, parfyt and trye.   80
Put thi trust in Godes mercye,
Hit is the beste at al assay,
And euer among thou the ennuye
Into this world and yusterday.

Sum men seith that deth is a thef   85
And al vnwarned wol on him stele,
And I sey nay and make a pref
That deth is studefast, trewe and lele,
And warneth vche mon of his greef
That he wol o day with him dele.   90
The lyf that is to ow so leof
He wol you reue and eke yor hele,
His poyntes may no mon him repele:
He cometh so baldely to pyke his pray—
When men beoth murgest at heor mele.   95
(I rede ye thenke on yusterday.)

48   *I Hafe Set My Herte So Hye*   Before 1400

Bodley MS Douce 381, f. 20. Index 1311. Brown XIV, 129. For music, Stainer I, plate XX (facsimile), and II, 51–2 (transcript). The MS dates c. 1425 but the piece evidently from before 1400.

I hafe set my herte so hye,
Me likyt no loue that lowere ys;

92. yor: MS or

And alle the paynes that y may drye
Me thenk hyt do me good ywys.

For on that lorde that louid vs alle   5
So hertely haue I set my thowht,
Yt ys my ioie on hym to calle,
For loue me hath in balus browht.
Me thenk hyt do me good iwys.

49   *At a Sprynge Wel Vnder a Thorn*   End of 14 c.

A spring love song with the pregnant brevity of Poem 19. Thorn, well, maiden quickly establish place and moment; healing well provides lover's medicine, as lady is the bearer of true love. Only its setting in an exemplum *De Confessione* implies that the whole is a devotion to Our Lady. In contrast see the opening of Poem 81, where the connection is made explicit.

Oxf. Magdalen Coll. MS. 60, f. 214. Index 420. Brown XIV, 130.

At a sprynge wel vnder a thorn
Ther was bote of bale a lytel here aforn.
Ther bysyde stant a mayde
Fulle of loue ybounde.
Hose wol seche trwe loue   5
Yn hyr hyt schal be founde.

50   *Canticus Amoris*   End of 14 c.

A meditation on Mary *Mediatrix* and Queen of Heaven, which is as genre both Nocturnal Vision and lady's Complaint. The Complaint draws on the Passion and the Virgin's Assumption, just as the love which is its refrain is touched by the passion of the Song of Songs. Nocturnal Vision provides occasion for the musing masculine 'I' but the shift to Complaint keeps the Virgin at the emotional centre. Mary, at once man's mother and sister, treats of love in a family tie made intense by its figurative complexity (see, e.g., St. Anselm, *Oratio 52*, in Migne CLVIII, pp. 957–8), which yet permits her

48. **3.** MS dryue   **9.** me good: *supplied*

to voice the reason for her complaint—man's flight from God—movingly as a
son's neglect of a woman's yearning devotion. For another view see Woolf,
pp. 301–2. *Cf* Poem 82.

Bodley MS Douce 322, ff. 8ᵛ–9ᵛ. Index 1460. Brown XIV 132.

> In a tabernacle of a toure,
> As I stode musyng on the mone,
> A crouned quene most of honoure
> Apered in gostly syght ful sone.
> She made compleynt thus by hyr one   5
> For mannes soule, was wrapped in wo;
> 'I may not leue mankynde allone,
> Quia amore langueo.
>
> 'I longe for loue of man, my brother,
> I am hys voket to voyde hys vyce;   10
> I am hys moder, I can none other,
> Why shuld I my dere chyld dispyce?
> Yef he me wrathe in diuerse wyse,
> Through flesshes freelte fall me fro,
> Yet must me rewe hym tyll he ryse,   15
> Quia amore langueo.
>
> 'I byd, I byde in grete longyng;
> I loue, I loke when man woll craue;
> I pleyne for pyte of peynyng;
> Wolde he aske mercy, he shuld hit have.   20
> Say to me, soule, and I shal saue,
> Byd me my chylde and I shall go;
> Thow prayde me neuer but my son forgaue,
> Quia amore langueo.
>
> 'O wreche, in the worlde I loke on the,   25
> I se thy trespas day by day,
> With lechery ageyns my chastite,
> With pryde agene my pore aray.

14. MS Though   **15.** me: MS we

My loue abydeth, thyne ys away;
My loue the calleth, thow stelest me fro.   30
Sewe to me, synner, I the pray,
Quia amore langueo.

'Moder of mercy I was for the made,
Who nedeth hit but thow allone?
To gete the grace I am more glade   35
Than thow to aske hit. Why wilt thou noon?
When seyed I nay, tel me, tyll oon?
Forsoth neuer yet to frende ne foo.
When thou askest nought then make I moone,
Quia amore langueo.   40

'I seke the in wele and wrechednesse,
I seke the in ryches and pouerte.
Thow man, beholde where thy moder ys,
Why louest thou me nat syth I loue the?
Synful or sory now euere thow be,   45
So welcome to me there are no mo.
I am thy suster, ryght trust on me,
Quia amore langueo.

'My childe ys outlawed for thy synne,
Mankynde, ys bette for thys trespasse;   50
Yet prykketh myne hert that so ny my kynne
Shuld be dysseased. O sone, allasse,
Thow art hys brother, hys moder I was;
Thow sokyd my pappe, thow louyd man so
Thow dyed for hym, myne hert he has,   55
Quia amore langueo.

'Man, leue thy synne than for my sake.
Why shulde I gyf the that thou nat wolde?
And yet yef thow synne some prayere take
Or trust in me as I have tolde.   60

31. MS shewe   50. thys: MS hys

Am nat I thy moder called?
Why shulde thou flee me? I loue the soo.
I am thy frende; I helpe, beholde,
Quia amore langueo.'

'Now sone,' she sayde, 'wylt thou sey nay   65
What man wolde mende hym of hys mys?
Thow lete me neuer in veyne yet pray.
Than, synfull man, see thow to thys.
What day thou comest, welcome thow ys,
Thys hundreth yere yef thow were fro.   70
I take the ful fayne, I clyppe, I kysse,
Quia amore langueo.

'Now wol I syt and sey nomore,
Leue and loke with grete longyng;
When man woll calle I wol restore.   75
I loue to saue hym, he ys myne hosprynge,
No wonder yef myne hert on hym hynge;
He was my neyghbore: what may I doo?
For hym had I thys worshippyng
And therefore amore langueo   80

'Why was I crouned and made a quene?
Why was I called of mercy the welle?
Why shuld an erthly woman bene
So hygh in heuen aboue aungelle?
For the, mankynde, the truthe I telle: 85
Thou aske me helpe and I shall do
That I was ordeyned, kepe the fro helle,
Quia amore langueo.

'Nowe man, haue mynde on me foreuer,
Loke on thy loue thus languysshyng.   90
Late vs neuer fro other disseuere,
Myne helpe ys thyne oune, crepe vnder my wynge.

62. thou ... me ... soo: MS I ... the ... loo

Thy syster ys a quene, thy brother ys a kynge,
Thys heritage ys tayled; sone come therto:
Take me for thy wyfe and lerne to synge   95
Quia amore langueo.'

51   *Nam Deus Non Verborum sed*   Late 14/15 c.
                        Cordis Est Auditor

   The English verses occur in the as yet unpublished Franciscan compilation
Fasciculus Morum I, vii, 'De Membris Superbie'. Written in the 14 c., the treatise
underwent revision, including the addition of many English poems, none of
which appears in the earlier MSS. See A. G. Little, *Studies in English Franciscan
History* (Manchester, 1917), especially pp. 139–41, and F. A. Foster, 'Some
English Words from the "Fasciculus Morum" ', *Essays and Studies in Honour of
Carleton Brown* (1940), especially p. 149, *n.* 2.
Bodley MS Rawlinson C670, f. 13. Index *2298.* For Latin, *Walther*, Sprichwörter
18723.

               Non uox sed uotum,
               Non musica cordula sed cor,
               Non clamor sed amor
               Sonat in aure Dei.

          Ne monnes steuen but gode wylle,   5
          No mirthe of mouth but herte stylle,
          No cry but love ne other bere
          Nys mirthe ny songe God to here.

52   *Mary Moder of Grace*   Late 14/15 c.

   A prayer to Mary *Mediatrix* and all the saints from the *Fasciculus Morum* I,
ix, 'Quibus Est Humiliandum': *cf* Brown *XV*, 124, and see Poem 51 and its
commentary.
Bodley MS Rawlinson C670, f. 15ᵛ. Index *2114. See Robbins in* Modern Philology
XXXVI, p. 345.

Maria mater gracie, mater misericordie, tu nos ab hoste protege in hora, etc.

Mary moder of grace, we cryen to the,
Moder of mercy and of pyte.
Wyte vs fro the fendes sondyng
• And helpe ves at oure last endynge,
And to thy sone oure pes thu make   5
That he on vs no wreche take.
Alle the halewen that aren in heuen,
To yow I crye with mylde steuene.
Helpe that Cryst my gult foryeue
And I wol him serue whyl that I leue.   10

53   *Regina Celi Letare*   Late 14/15 c.

From a 15 c. MS of the *Fasciculus Morum*: see commentary to Poem 51.
The text is preceded by an account of its relation to the antiphon of its title:
'Note that in this antiphon the alleluya is given in 4 ways, that is that here
there are 4 alleluyas. For one alleluya means the same as *lauda deum creatura*,
another *lux, vita et laus*, another *saluum ne fac deus*, and the fourth *pater et filius
et spiritus sanctus*.'

Bodley MS Laud Misc. 213, fol. 186. Index *2789*. Brown XV, *27*. Walther,
Initia *16516*.

Quene of heuen, mak thu murth
And prays God with all thi myght,
For of the he tok hys burth
That is heele, lyf and lyght.

He rose fro deth, so sayd he;   5
Save vs, Gode, in nede most.
Pray for vs the Trinite,
Fader and Sone and Holy Gost.

54   *Homo, Vide Quid Pro Te Pacior*   Late 14/15 c.

From the *Fasciculus Morum* III, x, 'Circa Modum Sue Passionis', in the section
on *Caritas* as the remedy for envy: see the commentary to Poem 51. The English
is one of several versions of the Latin, which, sometimes ascribed to St Bernard,

is by the Chancellor Philippe de Grève: See B. Hauréau, *De Poèmes Latins Attribués à Saint Bernard* (Paris, 1890), p. 76.

Bodley MS Rawlinson C670, f. 45ᵛ. Index 495. Walther, Initia 8401.

> *Homo, vide quid pro te pacior,*
> *Si est dolor sicut quo crucior.*
> *Ad te clamo qui pro te morior.*
> *Vide penas quibus afficior,*
> *Vide claues quibus confodior.*
> *Cum sit dolor tantus exterior,*
> *Interior autem planctus grauior*
> *Tam ingratum dum te experior.*

> Byholde, mon, what I dree,
> Whech is my payne, qwech is my woo.
> To the I clepe now I shal dye,
> Byse the wel for I mot go.
> Byholde the nayles that ben withoute,   5
> How they me thorles to thys tre.
> Of all my pyne haue I no doute
> But yif vnkynde I fynde the.

55   *O Vos Omnes Qui Transitis per Viam*   Late 14/15 c.

In this quatrain on the Passion the image is that of a wayside shrine from which the Crucified Christ speaks in the words of *Lamentations* I. 12. Several other similar quatrains, Latin and English, end with an exhortation *ad contemnendum mundum* (Woolf, p. 322 and Walther, *Initia* 13072), which is here put aside for the theme of love and suffering, as also in the *Homo, Vide Quid Pro Te Pacior*: see Poems 54 and 34. For a contrasting use of Lamentations as *memento mori* see Poem 101 and its commentary.

From the *Fasciculus Morum* III, x: see commentary to Poem 54.

Bodley MS Rawlinson C670, f. 45ᵛ. Index 2596.

> A ye men that by me wenden,
> Abydes a while and loke on me,
> Yef ye fynden in any ende
> Such soraw as here ye se on me.

56   *Wreche Mon, Why Art Thou Prowde?*   Late 14/15 c.

A *memento mori* from *Fasciculus Morum* I, xiii, 'Memoria Mortis Inducit
Humilitatem', where it is introduced by a passage from Gregory:
Mens sancti viri semper dolore et fletu afficitur considerando bene

> vbi fuit quia in peccato,
> vbi est quia in miseria,
> vbi non est quia in nulla gloria,
> vbi erit quia in iudicio timens de vindicta.

And another MS, Laud Misc. III, f. 65, adds on its lower margin *Versus de
Miseria Hominis:*

> Est ve nascendo, ve nato, ve moriendo,
> In amando suo ve: non viuit filius Eue.

Bodley MS Rawlinson C670, f. 20. Index 4239. Brown XIV, 133.

*Mens sancti viri semper dolere et fletu afficitur considerando bene vbi fuit
quia in peccato, vbi est quia in miseria, vbi non est quia in nulla gloria, vbi
erit quia in iudicio timens de vindicta; et ideo dicitur Anglice sic:*

> Wreche mon, why art thou prowde
> That art of erthe maket?
> Hedure ne brouhtest thou no schroude
> But pore thou come and naket.
> When thy soule is faren out   5
> Of thy body, with erthe yraket,
> That body that was so ronke and loud
> Of alle men is hated.

57   *Sephulchrum Clerici Diuiti Parisini*   Late 14/15 c.

Verses on the cynicism of executors of estates, by a rich and famous Paris
scholar, inscribed on the highly sculptured figurative funerary monument
ordered by him, with instructive irony, while still alive. From *Fasciculus Morum*
I, xiii, which also gives the French version.

Bodley MS Rawlinson C670, f. 21. Index 3863.

7. MS thas was

Pro epitaphio fecit depingi ymaginem sui ipsius, ad cuius pedes etiam depinxit
genus nummorum decurrencium in ciuitate aut terra. Ad caput autem et ex
vtraque parte dicte ymaginis fecit depingi suos executores . . . , quorum

> *Primus:* We ben executors of this dede,
> But of this monė what is our rede?
>
> *Secundus:* Take to the and I to me,
> The dede kepes of no monė.
>
> *Tercius:* By vs oure dyner whoso wol,   5
> The dede schal quyten al at the fulle.

58   *Kyng I Syt, Kynge I Was, I Shal Be Kynge:*   Late 14/15 c.

Rota a Domina Fortuna Reuoluta

Another mortuary piece from *Fasciculus Morum* IV, ii. illustrating the theme
'mortus sepelire mortuos' ('let the dead bury the dead'), it uses the *topos* of
kingship and Fortune's Wheel. The Latin original is itself an expansion of the
verbal tags commonly found on illustrations of the Wheel (see H. R. Patch,
The Goddess Fortuna [Cambridge, Mass., 1927], especially pp. 164–6):

> [Primus:]
> Rex presens regno,
> Fore cras sine regno.
>
> Secundus:
>   Heu mihi, regnaui,
> Quid prodest id quod amaui.
>
> Tercius:
> Nuper diues ego,
> Vix mea membra tego.
>
> Quartus:
> Sum regnaturus,
> Cum sim miser moriturus.

57. **3.** 'Take care of your part and I'll take care of mine' (with a double
entendre?)

Bodley MS Rawlinson C670, f. 72. Index *1822.*

> *Sic primus rex Anglice:*
> Kyng I syt and loke aboute,
> Tomorn I may ben withoute.

> *Secundus:*
> Wo is me, a kynge I was;   5
> This world I louede but that I las.

> *Tercius:*
> Nouhth longe gon I was ful ryche
> But nowe is ryche and pore ylyche.

> *Quartus:*
> I shal be kynge, that men schulle se   10
> When the wreche ded shal be.

---

59   *Longe Slepers and Ouer Lepers*   Late 14/15 c.

A piece on lazy and dancing clerics, from *Fasciculus Morum* V, iii, the section on *Accidia.* For a Latin version see *Rel. Antiq.* I, 90, though none appears in this MS.

Bodley MS Rawlinson C670, f. 90. Index *1935. Little,* English Franciscan History, *p. 153.*

> Longe slepers and ouer lepers,
> For skyppers and ouer hyppers,
> I holde luther hyne.
> I am noht heren
> Ne they ben myne.   5
> But they sone amende
> They shullen to helle pyne.

58. **1.** rex: *supplied*   59. **3.** MS luth

Secular Poems of the Fourteenth Century

60 *Icham of Irlaunde* Earlier 14 c.

This song and dance, written together with Poems 61 and 62 on a vellum scrap bound in the present MS, is thought to be one of the earliest carols: Greene, p. xxxvi.

Bodley MS. Rawlinson D. 913, f. 1ᵛ, item 7. Index 1008.

> Icham of Irlaunde
> Ant of the holy londe
> Of Irlande.
>
> Gode sire, pray ich the,
> For of saynte charite,   5
> Come ant daunce wyt me
> In Irlaunde.

61 *Al Nist by the Rose* 14 c.

In this and the four following poems the singing quality is evident though poetic differences are considerable. All employ 'popular' devices but are of the utmost sophistication. The present song by use of the rose image, by repetition of the word itself and simplicity of language, leads the reader into the gentle world of nature, only to turn the meaning at the end by skilful *double entendre*.

Bodley MS Rawlinson D. 913, fol. 1ᵛ, item 10. Index 194. Robbins Sec. XIV–XV, 17.

> Al nist by the rose, rose,
> Al nist bi the rose I lay.
> Darf ich noust the rose stele
> And yet ich bar the flour away.

60. 4. MS ye

62   *Maiden in the Mor Lay*   Earlier 14 c.

Incremental repetition and refrain produce the disclosure of this poem but
what is disclosed beyond the romantic reality is not within the limits of proper
inference; and those who here find in allegory the world as wilderness before
Christ's Coming (D. W. Robertson, 'Historical Criticism', *English Institute
Essays, 1950* [New York, 1951]) are simply doing what other good Christians
have done before them to 'sinful songs', writing, rather less lyrically than the
poet, a metaphoric stanza of their own like that of the 16 c. lyric *Come Over
the Borne, Bessye:* see commentary to Poem 49.

Bodley MS. Rawlinson D. 913, f. 1ᵛ, item 8. Index 3891. Robbins Sec. XIV–XV,
18.

> Maiden in the mor lay,
> In the mor lay,
> Seuenyst fulle,
> Seuenyst fulle.
> Maiden in the mor lay,   5
> In the mor lay,
> Seuenistes fulle ant a day.
>
> Welle was hire mete,
> Wat was hire mete?
> The primerole ant the,   10
> The primerole ant the.
> Welle was hire mete,
> Wat was hire mete?
> The primerole ant the violet.
>
> Welle was hire dryng,   15
> Wat was hire dryng?
> The chelde water of the,
> The chelde water of the.
> Well was hire dryng,
> Wat was hire dryng?   20
> The chelde water of the welle spring.

8. Welle: MS wat   15. was . . . dryng: *supplied*

Welle was hire bour.
Wat was hire bour?
The rede rose an te
The rede rose an te.   25
Welle was hire bour
Wat was hire bour?
The rede rose an te lilie flour.

63   *Me Thingkit Thou Art So Loueli*   14 c.

A simple statement by the speaker of premise and conclusion without *significatio* or metaphor.

BM MS Harley 7322, f. 162ᵛ. Index 2141. Robbins Sec. XIV-XV, 142.

Me thingkit thou art so loueli
So fair and so swete,
That sikerli it were mi det
Thi companie to lete.

64   *Bryd one Brere*   14 c.

A song with music uniting a lover's praise of his lady with a nature theme that might have been refrain or burden ('Bryd on brere'). Here the lover petitions, not the lady but the bird, seeking its aid: it is love which makes all nature one and the lover the bird's relation (line 2.) The carefully wrought verses, formed to fit the music, combine rhyme with alliteration, repetition and *annominatio* (line 5).

Camb. King's Coll. MS Muniment Roll 2 W. 32ᵛ. Index 521. Robbins Sec. XIV-XV, 147.

Bryd one brere, brid, brid one brere,
Kynd is come of loue, loue to craue.
Blithful biryd, on me thu rewe
Or greyth, lef, greid thu me my graue.

17–20, 24–7. *supplied*   64. **3.** MS blidful   64. **4.** greyth: MS greyd

Hic am so blithe, so bryhit, brid on brere,   5
Quan I se that hende in halle.
Yhe is quit of lime, loueli, trewe,
Yhe is fayr and flur of all.

Mikte hic hire at wille hauen,
Stedefast of loue, loueli, trewe,   10
Of mi sorwe yhe may me sauen,
Ioye and blisse were me newe.

65   *My Lefe Ys Faren in a Lond*   14 c.

Though written here in a later MS, this song was known to Chaucer:
Nun's Priest's Tale, lines 113–5 (B. lines 4067–9).

Camb. Trinity Coll. MS 599, f. 154. Index *2254. Robbins* Sec. XIV-XV, *160.*

My lefe ys faren in a lond.
Allas, why ys she so?
And I am so sore bound
I may not com her to.
She hath my hert in hold   5
Where euer she ryde or go
With trew love a thousand fold.
     Explicit.

66   *Alysoun*   Before 1340

A lover's springtime song of praise of his lady's perfections, the contempla-
tion of which accompanies his love-longing, The praise is also a convention of
the current amatory verse, but the lady's name is English, her virtues are un-
touched by literary metaphor, and the language especially of the refrain has
an idiosyncratic charm. See Poem 68 and its commentary.

BM MS Harley 2253, f. 63ᵛ. Index *515. Brown* XIII, *77. Brook 4. EETS 255*
(*facsimile*).

Bytuene Mersh ant Aueril
When spray biginneth to springe,

12. MS were were

The lutel foul hath hire wyl
On hyre lud to synge.
Ich libbe in louelonginge   5
For semlokest of all thynge;
He may me blisse bringe;
Icham in hire baundoun.
     An hendy hap ichabbe yhent,
     Ichot from heuene it is me sent;   10
     From alle wymmen mi loue is lent
     Ant lyht on Alysoun.

On heu hire her is fayr ynoh,
Hire browe broune, hire eye blake;
With lossum chere he on me loh,   15
With middel smal ant wel ymake.
Bote he me wolle to hire take
Forte buen hire owen make
Longe to lyuen ichulle forsake
Ant feye fallen adoun.   20
     An hendy hap, etc.

Nihtes when y wende ant wake
(Forthi my wonges waxeth won),
Leuedi, al for thine sake
Longinge is ylent me on.   25
In world nis non so wyter mon
That al hire bounte telle con.
Hire swyre is whittore then the swon,
Ant feyrest may in toune.
     An hendi, etc.   30

Icham for wowyng al forwake,
Wery so water in wore,
Lest eny reue me my make
Ychabbe y-yyrned yore.

30. MS hend

---

7. *He*, she

Betere is tholien whyle sore   35
Then mournen euermore.
Geynest vnder gore,
Herkne to my roun.
    An hendi, etc.

67   *Lenten Ys Come With Loue to Toune*   Before 1340

A lover's description of spring, richer and more fragrant in detail than any
other of its period. Less ebullient than Poem 17 (*Sumer is icumen in*), it is touched
by the conventional longing of a speaker whose amused wit is, however,
unconventional ('Wormes woweth vnder cloude, / Wymmen waxeth wounder
proude'). Stanza form and alliteration are the work of a poet as elegant as the
lover himself, and the words, as English as they can be, are also in a poetic
language destined to appear in courtly circles subsequently: see *University of
Toronto Quarterly* XXXIII (1964), pp. 269–72.

BM MS Harley 2253, f. 71ᵛ, col. 1. Index 1861. Brown XIII, 81. Brook 11.
EETS 255 (*facsimile*).

Lenten ys come with loue to toune,
With blosmen ant with briddes roune,
That al this blisse bryngeth.
Dayeseyes in this dales,
Notes suete of nyhtegales,   5
Vch foul song singeth.
The threstelcoc him threteth oo,
Away is huere wynter wo
When woderoue springeth.
This foules singeth ferly fele   10
Ant wlyteth on huere wynne wele
That al the wode ryngeth.

The rose rayleth hire rode,
The leues on the lyhte wode

11. wynne: MS wynter

---

37. 'Kindest in a gown', i.e. Alysoun
7. 'The thrush keeps bickering to himself'

Waxen al with wille.   15
The mone mandeth hire bleo,
The lilie is lossom to seo,
The fenyl ant the fille.
Wowes this wilde drakes,
Miles murgeth huere makes   20
Ase strem that striketh stille.
Mody meneth, so doth mo
(Ichot ycham on of tho),
For loue that likes ille.

The mone mandeth hire lyht,   25
So doth the semly sonne bryht
When briddes singeth breme.
Deawes donketh the dounes,
Deores wis'th huere derne rounes
Domes forte deme.   30
Wormes woweth vnder cloude,
Wymmen waxeth wounder proude
So wel hit wol hem seme.
Yef me shal wonte wille of on,
This wunne weol y wole forgon   35
Ant wyht in wode be fleme.

68   *Blow, Northerne Wynd*   Before 1340

This carol, in which a lover praises his lady, is both like and unlike Poem 66. Lines 15–30, though 'literary', are direct, but 31–8 employ the best-known similes of excellence from the contemporary love poetry, and 39–62 elaborate a dialogue with Love about Sighing, Thought and Sorrow, all in prosopopoeia.

22. MS doh
29. wis'th- = wiseth; MS with, *which all editors read as preposition. See paraphrase below*

22. *Mody meneth* 'The unhappy man makes (or sings) a complaint'
29–30. Lit. 'Beasts devise their dark runes to judge dooms', meaning perhaps 'Beasts contrive their cries incomprehensible to us, to tell their tales'

The burden 'Blow, northerne wynd', however, has the ring of popular song
and may be from that source.

*BM MS Harley 2253, ff. 72ᵛ, col. 1–73, col. 1. Index 1395. Brown XIII, 83.
Brook 14. Greene 440. EETS 255 (facsimile).*

> Blow, northerne wynd,
> Sent thou me my suetyng,
> Blow, northerne wynd,
> Blou, blou, blou!

Ichot a burde in boure bryht   5
That sully semly is on syht,
Menskful maiden of myht,
Feir ant fre to fonde.
In al this wurliche won
A burde of blod ant of bon   10
Neuer yete y nuste non
Lussomore in londe.
  Blow, etc.

With lokkes lefliche ant longe,
With frount ant face feir to fonde,   15
With murthes monie note heo monge,
That brid so breme in boure,
With lossom eye grete ant gode,
With browen blysfol vnder hode.
He that reste him on the rode   20
That leflich lyf honoure.
  Blou, etc.

Heo is dereworthe in day,
Gracious, stout ant gay
Gentil, iolyf so the iay,   25
Worhliche when heo waketh.
Maiden murgest of mouth

10. A living girl; *cf* Poem 18, line 10: *beste of bon and blod;* and Poem 33, lines
7–8: *Bestis and thos foules, the fisses in the flode, /And euch schef aliues imakid of
bone and blode*

D

Bi est, bi west, by north ant south
Ther nis fiele ne crouth
That such murthes maketh.   30

Heo is coral of godnesse,
Heo is rubie of ryhtfulnesse,
Heo is cristal of clannesse
Ant baner of bealte.
Heo is lilie of largesse,   35
Heo is paruenke of prouesse,
Heo is solsecle of suetnesse
Ant ledy of lealte.

To Loue, that leflich is in londe,
Y tolde him, as ych vnderstonde,   40
Hou this hende hath hent in honde
On huerte that myn wes,
Ant hire knyhtes me han so soht,
Sykyng, Sorewyng ant Thoht,
Tho thre me han in bale broht   45
Ayeyn the poer of Pees.

To Loue y putte pleyntes mo,
Hou Sykyng me hath siwed so
Ant eke Thoht me thrat to slo
With maistry, yef he myhte,   50
Ant Serewe sore in balful bende
That he wolde for this hende
Me lede to my lyues ende
Vnlahfulliche in lyhte.

Hire Loue me lustnede vch word   55
Ant beh him to me ouer bord
Ant bed me hente that hord
Of myne huerte hele,
'Ant bisecheth that swete ant swote,
Er then thou falle ase fen of fote,   60
That heo with the wolle of bote
Dereworthliche dele.'

For hire loue y carke ant care,
For hire loue y droupne ant dare,
For hire loue my blisse is bare,   65
Ant al ich waxe won.
For hire loue in slep y slake,
Fore hire loue al nyht ich wake,
For hire loue mournyng y make
More then eny mon.   70

---

69   *De Clerico et Puella*   Before 1340

This poem reflects the conventions of two interrelated genres—the medieval
conflictus or *debate* (Winter and Summer, Owl and Nightingale, Student and
Bird), which in turn goes back to the classical eclogue; and the French *pastourelle*,
in which knightly male tries to persuade or force maiden, who avoids surrender
by a promise and the actual intervention of male relatives, or postpones it by
promise and threatened intervention. As in *conflictus* the student sweet-talks
his way to victory ('thou spekest so scille'), but as sometimes in *pastourelle*
the moral is that she's done all this before. See H. Walther, *Das Streitgedicht
in d. lat. lit. des Mittelalters* (München, 1920) and W. P. Jones, *The Pastourelle*
(Cambridge, Mass., 1931).

*BM MS Harley 2253, f. 80ᵛ. Index 2236. Brown XIII, 85. Brook 24. EETS 255
(facsimile).*

'My deth y loue, my lyf ich hate, for a leuedy shene;
Heo is briht so daies liht, that is on me wel sene;
Al y falewe so doth the lef in somer when hit is grene.
Yef mi thoht helpeth me noht, to wham shal y me mene?

'Sorewe ant syke ant drery mod byndeth me so faste   5
That y wene to walke wod yet hit me lengore laste.
My serewe, my care, al with a word heo myhte awey caste.
Whet helpeth the, my suete lemmon, my lyf thus forte gaste?'

'Do wey, thou clerc, thou art a fol, with the bydde y noht chyde.
Shalt thou neuer lyue that day mi loue that thou shalt byde.   10

2. MS brith   7. heo: he MS

Yef thou in my boure art take, shame the may bityde.
The is bettere on fote gon then wycked hors to ryde.'

'Weylawei! Whi seist thou so? Thou rewe on me, thy man.
Thou art euer in my thoht in londe wher ich am.
Yef y deye for thi loue hit is the mykel sham.   15
Thou lete me lyue ant be thi luef ant thou my suete lemman.'

'Be stille, thou fol (y calle the riht); cost thou neuer blynne?
Thou art wayted day ant nyght with fader ant all my kynne.
Be thou in mi bour ytake, lete they for no synne
Me to holde ant the to slon; thi deth so thou maht wynne.'   20

'Suete ledy, thou wend thi mod, sorewe thou wolt me kythe.
Ich am al so sory mon so ich was whylen blythe.
In a wyndou ther we stod we custe vs fyfty sythe.
Feir biheste maketh mony mon al is serewes mythe.'

'Weylawey! Whi seist thou so? Mi serewe thou makest newe.   25
Y louede a clerk al par amours, of loue he wes full trewe.
He nes nout blythe neuer a day bot he me sone seye.
Ich louede him betere then my lyf, whet bote is hit to leye?'

'Whil y wes a clerc in scole, wel muchel y couthe of lore.
Ych haue tholed for thy loue woundes fele sore   30
Fer from hom ant eke from men vnder the wodegore.
Suete ledy, thou rewe of me. Nou may y no more.'

'Thou semest wel to ben a clerc, for thou spekest so scille.
Shalt thou neuer for mi loue woundes thole grylle.
Fader, moder ant al my kun ne shal me holde so still   35
That y nam thyn ant thou art myn, to don al thi wille.'

17. MS riþt   20. thi: MS þe
31. hom *emended Brook, MS omitted*   33. MS stille

When the Nyhtegale Singes   Before 1340

Despite the English localism of line 17, this is the standard spring song of a
stricken lover, whose lady's kiss would be his medicine, as thought of her
makes him, like the April plants, wax green.

BM MS *Harley 2253, f. 80ᵛ*. Index *4037*. Brown. XIII. *86*. Brook *25*. EETS *255*
(*facsimile*).

When the nyhtegale singes the wodes waxen grene;
Lef ant gras and blosme springes in Aueryl, y wene.
Ant loue is to myn herte gon with one spere so kene,
Nyht ant day my blod hit drynkes; myn herte deth me tene.

Ich haue loued al this yer, that y may loue namore;   5
Ich haue siked moni syk, lemmon, for thin ore.
Me nis loue neuer the ner, ant that me reweth sore.
Suete lemmon, thench on me, ich haue loued the yore.

Suete lemmon, y preye the of loue one speche.
Whil y lyue in world so wyde other nulle y seche.   10
With thy loue, my suete leof, mi blis thou mihtes eche;
A suete cos of thy mouth mihte be my leche.

Suete lemmon, y preeye the of a loue bene:
Yef thou me louest ase men says, lemmon, as y wene,
Ant yef hit thi wille be, thou loke that hit be sene.   15
So muchel y thenke vpon the that al y waxe grene.

Bituene Lyncolne ant Lyndeseye, Northamptoun ant Lounde,
Ne wot y non so fayr a may as y go fore ybounde.
Suete lemmon, y preye the thou louie me a stounde.
Y wole mone my song on wham that hit ys on ylong.   20

18. *go fore ybounde:* 'go in fetters for'
20. 'I shall sadly sing my song about the one on whom it is dependent,' i.e.
'about the one who is its cause'

Hou Derne Loue May Stonde   Before 1340

This poem, a companion piece to Poem 29, is a tissue of Courtly Love commonplaces: the love is secret, hence the lady may not be named (lines 2, 9–10); the lover sues for the lady's 'grace' (lines 16–19), without which he will be in desperate straits (line 21); the lover is faithful and zealous (lines 7–8) but the lady is stand-offish (line 14). That she is also variable and faithless (lines 5, 27, 34)—a commonplace of anti-feminist satire and a topic of love among the troubadours (*amars*, as distinct from *fin amour*)—suggests the stress of the religious moralist contrasting worldly love with love of Christ.

BM MS Harley 2253, f. 128. Index *1921.* Brown XIII, *91.* Brook 32. *EETS 255* (*facsimile*).

Lutel wot hit any mon
Hou derne loue may stonde,
Bote hit were a fre wymmon
That muche of loue had fonde.
The loue of hire ne lesteth nowyht longe;   5
Heo haueth me plyht ant wyteth me wyth wronge.
Euer ant oo for my leof icham in grete thohte;
Y thenche of hire that y ne seo nout ofte.

Y wolde nemne hyre today
Ant y dorste hire munne;   10
Heo is that feireste may
Of vch ende of hire kunne.
Bote heo me loue, of me heo haues sunne.
Who is him that loueth the loue that he ne may ner ywyne.
Euer ant oo, etc.   15

Adoun y fel to hire anon
Ant crie, 'Ledy, thyn ore!
Ledy, ha mercy of thy mon,
Lef thou no false lore.
Yef thou dost, hit wol me reowe sore.   20
Loue dreccheth me that y ne may lyue namore.'
Euer ant oo, etc.

Mury hit ys in hyre tour
Wyth hatheles ant wyth heowes.
So hit is in hyre bour,   25
With gomenes ant with gleowes.
Bote heo me louye, sore hit wol me rewe.
Wo is him that loueth the loue that ner nul be trewe.
Euer ant oo, etc.

Ffayrest fode vpo loft,   30
My gode luef, y the greete
Ase fele sythe ant oft
As dewes dropes beth weete,
Ase sterres beth in welkne ant grases sour ant suete.
Whose loueth vntrewe, his herte is selde seete.   35
Euer ant oo, etc.

72   *Dronken*   14 c. (?)

A drunkard to himself and other drinkers drunkenly, in a copy hard to con because of fading. The editor has reread the poem standing on his head and apologizes if it seems in any sense more sober.

*Bodley MS Rawlinson d. 913, f. 1ᵛ, item 12. Index *24. Robbins Sec. XIV-XV, 117.*

    D . . . . . . dronken, dronken,
    Dronken, dronken, ydronken;
    Dronkcn is Tabart,
    Dronken is Tabart atte wyne,
    Hay!   5
    Ye haveth al ydronken,
    Suster, Walter, Peter,
    Ye dronke al depe
    Ant ichulle eke.
    Stondet alle stille,   10

MS *faded; the following insertions, made with aid of ultra-violet lamp, are conjectural:*
1. [dronken] dronken   **3.** [Dronken is T] ab [art]   **6.** [h] a [veth] a [l]

Stille, stille, stille,
Stondet alle stille,
Stille as any ston.
Trippe a lutel wit thi fot
Ant let thi body go.   15

73   *Wer Ther Outher in This Toun Ale or Wyn*   14 c.

Bodley MS Rawlinson d. 913, f. 1ᵛ, item 9. Index 3898. Robbins Sec. XIV-XV,
9.

Wer ther outher in this toun
Ale or wyn,
Isch hit wolde bugge
To lemmon myn.
Welle wo was so hardy   5
Forte make my lef al blody;
Thaut he were the kynges sone
Of Normaundy,
Yet icholde awreke boe
For lemman myn.   10

Welle wo was me tho,
Wo was me tho:
The man that leset that he louit
Hym is also.
Ne erle ne lerde   15
Ne—no more I n'can!
But Crist ich hire biteche
That was my lemman.

74   *Go, Peni, Go*   14 c.

Camb. Caius Coll. MS 261, f. 234. Index 3209. Robbins Sec. XIV-XV, 60.

Spende and God schal sende,
Spare and ermor care.

73. **2.** MS wy

Non peni, non ware;
Non catel, non care.
Go, peni, go.   5

75   *That Y Spende*   Late 14/15 c.

Inscriptions on three (or four) rings found in an ancient sarcophagus; from *Fasciculus Morum* V, xx, which cites the *Gesta Romanorum*: see edition by H. Oesterley (Berlin, 1871), fasc. I, p. 300, and edition by W. Dick (Erlangen, 1890), p. 26. The idea goes back to a tomb inscription of Sardanapalus as quoted from Aristotle in Cicero's *Tusculanian Disputations*, V. xxv. 101, and the English lines often occur on funerary monuments later.

Bodley MS Rawlinson C670, f. 115ᵛ. Index 3275; cf. Supplement *1924.3.*

> *Quod expendi habui,*
> *Quod donaui habeo,*
> *Quod seruaui perdidi,*
> *Quod negaui punior.*

> That y spende that y had,   5
> That y yeue that y haue,
> That y kepte ys lost fro myne,
> For that I warnyt now ys pyne.

76   *To Take and Wedde The*   Late 14/15 c.

A betrothal oath, from *Fasciculus Morum* III, viii, 'Quomodo Caritas Sit Elongata.'

Bodley MS Rawlinson C670, f. 44. Index 565.

> *Me tibi nupturam sponsam comitemque futuram.*

> By dedes of dayne I swere to the
> Herafter to take and wedde the.

8. that *supplied*
   D*

77   *Trewe Loue*   Late 14/15 c.

From the same chapter of *Fasciculus Morum* as Poem 76.
Bodley MS Rawlinson C670, f. 41ᵛ. Index *3802*.

> Trewe loue among men that most is of lette
> In hattes, in hodes, in porses is sette.
> Trewe loue in herbers spryngeth in May,
> But trewe loue of herte went is away.

78   *Engelond May Synge Alas Alas*   Late 14/15 c.

A lamentation on the corruption of the times, from *Fasciculus Morum* IV,
iii, 'Circa Membra Auaricie et Cupiditatis'. Such complaints, going back to
ancient Rome, have their own English history from the 12ᵗʰ c.: e.g. Bernard
de Morlai, *De Contemptu Mundi*, in Wright, *The Anglo Latin Satirical Poets
and Epigrammatists* (1872), II, 40, 47, etc.
Bodley MS Rawlinson C670, f. 74ᵛ. Index *3133*.

> Sithyn law for wylle bygynnyt to slakyn
> And falsehed for sleythe is itakyn,
> Robbyng and reuynge ys holdyn purchas
> And of vnthewes is made solas,
> Engelond may synge, Alas, alas!   5

78. **2.** MS scheythe

Religious and Moral Poems of the Fifteenth Century

79 *I Syng A of a Myden That Is Makeles*   Earlier 15 c.

A much commented spring song. Its dew metaphor for the Nativity is traditional, but its incremental repetition produces that unfolding of the image which, together with the adverb 'stille', makes it the loveliest and gentlest poem on its subject in English. See, among others, B. C. Raw, in *MLR* LV (1960), pp. 411–4, S. Manning, in *PMLA* LXXV (1960), pp. 8–12, and Woolf pp. 242 and 286–7.

BM MS Sloane 2593, f. 10ᵛ. Index 1367. Brown XV, 81.

> I syng a of a myden that is makeles.
> Kyng of alle kyngis to her sone che ches.
>
> He cam also stylle ther his moder was
> As dew in Aprylle that fallyt on the gras.
>
> He cam also stylle to his moderis bowr   5
> As dew in Aprille that fallyt on the flour.
>
> He cam also stylle ther his moder lay
> As dew in Aprille that fallyt on the spray.
>
> Moder and maydyn was neuer non but che.
> Wel may swych a lady Godis moder be.   10

80 *Adam Lay Ibowndyn*   Earlier 15 c.

Reversal of expectation brings charm to this statement of the consequence of a crime, in a brief poem of praise for Mary. The theme is that *felix culpa* joyously acclaimed on Easter Eve: see Woolf, pp. 290–1.

BM MS Sloane 2593, f. 11. Index 117. Brown XV, 83.

Adam lay ibowndyn, bowndyn in a bond;
Fowre thowsand wynter thowt he not to long.
And al was for an appil, an appil that he tok,
As clerkis fyndyn wretyn in here book.

Ne hadde the appil take ben, the appil taken ben,   5
Ne hadde neuer our lady a ben heuene qwen.
Blyssid be the tyme that appil take was.
Therfore we mown syngyn, 'Deo gracias.'

81   *Out of the Blosme Sprang a Thorn*   Earlier 15 c.

A song for Epiphany. See Poem 49 and its commentary.
BM MS Sloane 2593, ff. 12–13ᵛ. Index 2730. Brown XV, 88.

Out of the blosme sprang a thorn
Quan God hymself wold be born
He let vs neuere be forlorn
That born was of Marie.

Ther sprang a welle al at here fot   5
That al this word it trnyd to good,
Quan Ihesu Cryst took fleych and blod
Of his moder Marie.

Out of the welle sprang a strem
Fro patriarch to Jerusalem   10
Til Cryst hymself ayen it nem
Of his moder Marie.

In wynter quan the frost hym fres
A powre beddyng our Lord hym ches:
Betwyin an ox and an as   15
Godis sone born he was
Of his moder Marie.

12. MS of his moder etc.   **17.** MS of his etc.

It was vpon the Twelwe Day
Ther come three kyngis in ryche aray
To seke Cryst ther he lay   20
And his moder Marie.

Thre kyngis out of dyuers londe
Swythe comyn with herte stronge
The chyld to sekyn and vnderfonge
That born was of Marie.   25

The sterre led hem a ryte way
To the chyld ther he lay.
He help vs bothe nyht and day
That born was of Marie.

Baltyzar was the ferste kyng,   30
He browte gold to his offeryng
For to presente that ryche kyng
And his moder Marie.

Melchiar was the secunde kyng,
He browte incens to his offering   35
For to presente that ryche kyng
And his moder Marie.

Jasper was the thred kyng,
He browte myrre to his offeryng
For to presente that ryche kyng   40
And his moder Marie.

Ther they offerid here presents
With gold and myrre and francincens,
As clerkis redyn in here seqwens
In Ephifanye.   45

Knel we down hym beforn

22. MS dyues   **21, 37, 41.** MS and his etc.
44. As: MS &   **45.** In *supplied*

And prey we to hym that now is born,
And let us neuer be forlorn
That born was of Marie.

A meditation on the Passion and on the Compassion of the Virgin in the shape of a carol. It is like Poem 50 in combining Vision and Complaint but unlike in its cryptic dream-like procedure, with the last line of the burden referring to the lady and the first three lines to the half awake 'I', whom the poem draws into the Complaint scene itself—thus cutting across vision and reality—and specifies as the 'man' of Mary's appeal. The theme remains the same, man's inability to love, but the poem's emotion is intensified by play between the Virgin's appeal to hard-hearted man, conceived of as her son, and her sobbing ('Now breke hert') over the corpse of that other child, her crucified son, which she kisses at the climax of the action.

*Manchester Rylands Lib. MS Lat. 395, f. 120*rv. Index 4189. Brown XV, 9. Greene 161.

> Sodenly afraide,
> Half wakyng, half slepyng,
> And gretly dismayed,
> A woman sate weepyng,

With fauoure in hir face ferr passyng my reason,   5
And of hir sore weepyng this was the encheson:
Hir soon in hir lap lay, she seid, slayne by treason.
Yif wepyng myght ripe bee it seemyd than in season.
'Ihesu,' so she sobbid,
So hir soon was bobbid   10
And of his lif robbid,
Saying thies wordis, as I say thee:
'Who cannot wepe come lerne at me.'

I said I cowd not wepe, I was so harde hartid.
Shee answered me with wordys shortly that smarted: 15
'Lo, nature shall move the, thou must be converted.
Thyne owne fader this nyght is deed.' Lo, thus she thwarted.

'So my soon is bobbid
And of his lif robbid.'
Forsooth than I sobbid,   20
Veryfying the wordis she seid to me:
Who cannot wepe may lern at the.

'Now breke hert, I the pray. This cors lith so rulye,
So betyn, so wowndid, entreted so Iewlye,
What wight may me behold and wepe nat? noon truly,   25
To see my deed dere soon lygh bleedyng, lo, this newlye'.
And still she sobbid
So hir soon was bobbid
And of his lif robbid,
Newyng the wordis, as I say thee: 30
'Who cannot wepe come lern at me.'

On me she caste hir ey, said, 'See, man, thy brothir.'
She kissid hym and said, 'Swete, am I not thy modir?'
In sownyng she fill there, it wolde be noon othir.
I not which more deedly, the toon or the tothir.   35
Yit she revived and sobbid,
So hir soon was bobbid
And of his lif robbid.
'Who cannot wepe,' this was the laye,
And with that word she vanysht away.   40

83   *O Farest Lady*   15 c.

In keeping with the *mediatrix* theme lines 14–23 repeat the ancient *motif*, found in various accounts of the otherworld, of the saintly intervention with God for a sinner at the time of death against the demons claiming 'something of their own'.

Edinburgh Univ. MS Laing 149. f. 4. Index *2557.* Brown XV, *20.*

> O farest lady, O swetast lady,
> O blisful lady, hewynnis quheyne.

27. MS An

O sterne so brycht
That gyfys lycht
Til hewyne and Haly Kirk,   5
Thi help, thi mycht
Grant ws ful rycht,
Raik throw thire clowdis dirk,
Fra Hel sa fel conwoy ws clene.
One the, Mare, thus most I meyne.   10

Thow ruby red
That rasis ded
And grantis synnarise thare lyf,
For til remeid
The fendis pleid   15
Quha can thi help discrif?
But the, lady, quha may sustene
Thare wardly lustis both scharp and kene?

Thow well of grace,
Ostend thi face   20
Quhen ded sal ws persew,
Away thow chase
Of fendis the brase,
Ask at thi sone Ihesu,
One ruyd his blud that bled betwene   25
For oure traspass before thin eyne.

Now, lady myne,
Thi ere inclyne
To me, thi seruitour.
Quhen I go hyne   30
Hef my saul fra pyne.
Thow keip it in this cwre
In place quhare grace ay growis grene
Foreuer in ioy thartil contein.

    A farest lady, O swetast lady,   35
    O blisful lady, hewynnis quheyne.

84   *Timor Mortis Conturbat Me*   Earlier 15 c.
                          By John Awdelay

One of many poems on the fear of death using the refrain from the Office
of the Dead (see Woolf, pp. 333–6), this carol is by the blind priest of Haghmon
Abbey in Shropshire, writing *c.* 1425. All the themes on man's vileness and
de contemptu mundi are commonplaces, as are the prayers to Christ by the
medicine of his wounds and to Mary by her joys: see Poem 103. But the ref-
erence to the poet's blindness, to the loss of his health and all his zest is personal
and moving.

Bodl. MS Douce 302, ff. 30ᵛ and 32. Index 693. Greene 369. Whiting, in EETS,
o.s. 184 (1931), pp. 211–12.

> Lade, helpe. Jhesu, merce.
> Timor mortis conturbat me.

> Dred of deth, sorrow of syn
> Trobils my hert ful greuysly.
> My soule hit nyth with my lust then.   5
> Passio Cristi conforta me.

> Fore blyndnes is a heue thyng
> And to be def therwith only,
> To lese my lyght and my heryng.
> Passio Cristi conforta me.   10

> And to lese my tast and my smellyng
> And to be seke in my body:
> Here haue I lost al my lykyng.
> Passio Cristi conforta me

> Thus God he yeues and takys away   15
> And as he wil so mot hit be.
> His name be blessid both nyght and daye.
> Passio Cristi conforta me.

Here is a cause of gret mornyng:
Of myselfe nothyng I se   20
Saue filth, vnclennes, vile stynkyng.
Passio Cristi conforta me.

Into this world no more I broght,
No more I gete with me trewly
Saue good ded, word, wil and thoght.   25
Passio Cristi conforta me.

The v wondis of Jhesu Crist
My midsyne now mot thai be
The fyndis pouere downe to cast.
Passio Cristi conforta me.   30

As I lay seke in my langure
With sorow of hert and teere of ye,
This caral I made with gret doloure.
Passio Cristi confronta me.

Oft with these prayere I me blest,   35
'In manus tuas, Domine;
Thou take my soule into thi rest.'
Passio Cristi conforta me.

Mare moder, merceful may,
Fore the joys thou hadist, lady,   40
To thi sun fore me thou pray.
Passio Cristi conforta me.

Lerne this lesson of blynd Awdlay:
When bale is hyest then bot may be.
Yif thou be nyd nyght or day,   45
Say, 'Passio Cristi conforta me.'

23. MS word

85   *O Swete Angell, Bryng Me to Blysse*   15 c.
                 A Praier to the Goode Angell

*Calif. Huntingdon Lib. MS Ellesmere 34. B. 7, fol. 81. Index 2560. Brown
XV, 134.*

    O swete angell, to me soo deere,
    That nyght and day standithe me neere
    Full loueyngly with mylde moode,
    Thankyng, loueyng, loue and praysyng.
    Offer for me to Ihesu our kyng   5
    For his gyfftes greate and goode.

    As thow gothe betwix hym and me
    And knowethe my lyffe in euery degre,
    Saying it in his presence,
    Aske me grace to loue hym truly,   10
    To serue my lorde with hertt duly,
    With my dayly diligence.

    Keepe me from vice and all perells
    Whiles thowe with me dayly trauells
    In this worlde of wyckednesse.   15
    Sett me my peticions grauntede
    By thy praier dayly haunted,
    Yff it please thy holynes.

    The versicull:
    O swete angell that keepith me,   20
    Bryng me to blysse, I pray the.

86   *It Is My Fader Wyll*   Mid 15 c. or after

    Another religious carol with its burden a lullaby, the child fretting about the
tragedy of his coming life and the mother interjecting a hush.
Bodl. MS Additional A. 106, ff. 14ᵛ–15. Index 1264. Brown XV, 3. Greene 147.

    'Lullay, lullay, my lityl chyld,
    Slepe and be now styll.

If thou be a lytill chyld
Yitt may thou haue thi wyll.'

'How suld I now, thou fayre may,   5
Fall apon a slep?
Better me thynke that I may
Fall apon and wepe.
For He that mad both nyght and day,
Cold and also hette,   10
Now layd I am in a wispe of hay,
I can noder go nor crepe.
Bot wel I wate, as well I may,
("Slepe and be now styll!")
Suffre the paynes that I may,   15
It is my Fader wyll.

'Seys thou noghte, thou fayr may,
And heris thou noghte also
How Kynge Herod, that keyn knyght,
And of his peres mo   20
That be abowte nyght and day
My body for to slo?
Thai seke me both nyght and day
That werke me mekyll wo.
Bot well I wate, as well I may,   25
("Slepe and be now styll!")
Suffre the paynes that I may,
It is my Fader wyll.

'How suld I now, thou fayr may,
How suld I now myrth make?   30
My songe is mad of walaway,
For dred I begyn to whake,
For dred of that ilk day
That I my deth sall take
And suffre the paynes that I may   35
For synfull man sake.

24, 34. That: MS *omits initial* t

For well I wate, as well I may,
("Slepe and be now styll!")
Suffre the paynes that I may,
It is my Fader wyll.   40

'Bot yitt me thynk it well besett
If man haue of me mynd,
And al my paynes well besett
If man to me be kynd.
Thar is no deth that sall me let,   45
And I hym trew fynd,
On the rode for to sytt,
My handis for to bynd.
Bot well I wat, as well I may,
("Slepe and be now styll!")   50
Suffre the paynes that I may,
It is my Fader wyll.'

<hr>

87   Viii *Is My Loue*   15 c.

A˹'cipher' poem.
Bodl. MS Douce 257, f. 77. Index *717.* *Robbins* Sec. XIV-XV, *82.*

Viii ys my loue
Yif ix go bifore.
Wer viii ygert aboue
Iii wer wel therfore.

<hr>

88   *Vpon My Ryght Syde Y Me Leye*   15 c.

BM MS Harley 541, f. 288ᵛ. Index *927.* *Brown* XV, *127.*

Vpon my ryght syde y me leye;
Blesid Lady, to the y pray
For the teres that ye lete

87. **1–4.** *ix* before *viii* and *viii* before *iii* = IHC, i.e. Ihesus

Vpon yowre swete sonnys feete.
Sende me grace for to slepe   5
And good dremys for to mete,
Slepyng, wakyng, til morowe daye bee.
Owre Lorde is the frwte, Oure Lady is the tree,
Blessid be the blossome that sprange, Lady, of the.
In nomine Patris et Filii et Spiritus Sancti.   10
                                          Amen.

89   *Trusty Messanger I The Sende*   15 c.

   Another poem to Mary using the conventions of secular love. Epistolary
formula, terms of eulogy, the commonplace or *topos* of inexpressibility, all
occur in contemporary amatory verse (see, e.g., Poems 126 and 141, and for
some of the language, 118 and 119), and belong with the traditions of epideictic
rhetoric, panegyric, *de laudibus et vituperandis*, as do all prayers to flatter a
magnate or a deity. The poem's power lies in its ambiguity, gently resolved
by line 17 (*mediatrix*) and in this light thereafter by line 32 (her virgin state
unique, hence inexpressible).

Bodley MS Douce 326, f. 14ʳᵛ. Index 927. Brown XV, 46,

        Goe, lytyll byll, and doe me recommende
        Vnto my lady with godely countynaunce,
        For trusty messanger I the sende.
        Pray her that sche make puruyaunce,
        For my loue thurgh her sufferaunce   5
        In her bosom desyreth to reste,
        Syth of all women I loue here beste.

        She ys lylly off redolence,
        Wych only may doe me plesure.
        She is the rose off conffydence,   10
        Most conffortyng to my nature.
        Vnto that lady I me assure
        I wyll hur loue and neuer mo.
        Goe, lytyll byll, and sey hur so.

        She restyd in my remembraunce   15

Day other nyght, wherso I be.
It ys my specyall dalyaunce
For to remembyr hur bewte.
She is enprentyd in ych degre
With yftis of nature inexplycable   20
And eke of grace incomparable.

The cause therfor, yf she wyll wytt,
Wy I presume on sych a flowre,
Say off hyr, for yt ys iwrytt,
She is the feyrest paramour   25
And to man in ych langour
Most souerayn medyatryce.
Therffor I loue that flowre of pryce.

Her bewte holy to dyscryve
Who is he that may suffyce?   30
Forsoth no clerk that is on lyve,
Syth she is only withowtyn vyce.
Her flauour excedith the flowr delyce.
Afore all flowris I haue hur chose
Enterely in myn herte to close.   35

Hyr I beseche, seth I not feyne
Butt only putt me in hur grace,
That off me she not dysdeyne,
Takyng regarde at old trespace,
Seth myn entent in euery place   40
Shall be to doe hur obeysaunce
And hur to loue saunce varyaunce.

90   *This World I See Is But a Chery Fayre*   15 c.

A piece on death and transiency in the shape of a Farewell. The themes are
commonplaces of the homiletic poetry, and the Farewell formula, also familiar,
occurs as well in the poetry of love: see Poem 143. But 'chery fayre' is striking

23. MS Wyll   **30.** he: MS she

(*cf* Brown *XIV*, 117, line 85) and so is the *Totentanz* figure of Death's chess game (compare the episode in Ingmar Bergman's *The Seventh Seal*). More important, the union of themes and formula in a dying man's speech gives them a fresh poetic form.

Oxf. Balliol MS 354, f. 199. Index 769. Brown XV, 149.

> Farewell this world, I take my leve for euer,
> I am arrestid to appere affore Godis face.
> O mercyfull God, Thow knowest that I had lever
> Than all this worldis good to haue an owre space
> For to make aseth for my gret trespace.   5
> My harte, alas, is brokyn for that sorow.
> Som be this day that shall not be tomorow.
>
> This world, I see, is but a chery fayre,
> All thyngis passith and so moste I algate.
> This day I satt full royally in a chayre   10
> Tyll sotyll deth knokkid at my gate
> And vnavised he said to me, 'Chekmate!'
> Loo, how sodynly he maketh a devorce
> And wormes to fede here he hath layde my corse.
>
> Speke softe, ye folkis, for I am layde a slepe.   15
> I haue my dreme, in triste is myche treason.
> From dethis hold fayn wold I make a lepe
> But my wisdom ys torned into feble reason:
> I see this worldis joye lastith but a season.
> Wold God I had remembrid this beforne!   20
> I say no more but beware of an horne.
>
> This febyll world, so false and so vnstable,
> Promoteth his lovers but for a lytill while,
> But at last he geveth them a bable
> Whan his payntid trowth is torned into gile.   25
> Experyence cawsith me the trowth to compile,
> Thynkyng this: to late, alas, that I began;
> For foly and hope disseyveth many a man.

Farewell my frendis, the tide abidith no man;
I moste departe hens and so shall ye,   30
But in this passage the beste songe that I can
Is Requiem Eternam. I pray God grant it me.
Whan I haue endid all myn adversite
Graunte me in paradise to haue a mancyon,
That shede his blode for my redempcion.   35
  Beati mortui qui in Domino morivntur.
  Humiliatus sum vermis.

91   *Go Day, Syre Cristemas,* Mid 15 c. or before
      Our Kyng

Poems 91–94 are carols for Christmas.

Bodley MS Arch. Selden B. 26, f. 8. Index 1004. Greene 5. For music see Stainer
I, plate xlvii (facsimile) and II, 107 (transcription).

   Go day, go day,
   My lord Syre Cristemasse, go day.

  Go day, Syre Cristemas our kyng,
  For euery man, both olde and yynge,
  Ys glad and blithe of your comynge.   5
    Go day.

  Godys sone so moche of myght
  Fram heuen to erthe dovn is lyght
  And borne ys of a mayde so bryght.
    Go day.   10

  Heuen and erthe and also helle
  And alle that euer in hem dwelle
  Of your comynge they beth full snelle.
    Go day.

  Of your comynge this clerkys fynde,   15
  Ye come to saue al mankynde

35. MS redempcon

And of here balys hem vnbynde.
    Go day.

Alle maner of merthes we wole make
And solas to oure hertys take,   20
My semely lorde, for youre sake.
    Go day.

92   *Nowel, Nowel, Nowel*   Mid 15 c. or after

MS *heading:* A song vpon (now must I syng etc.)

    Setting and development suggest the conventions of 'sinful songs' and *chansons d'adventure* (the pregnant and deserted girl: see Poems 22, 27, 109 and 114) adapted to the Nativity.

Bodley MS Eng. poet. e. 1, f. 47ᵛ. Index 3822. Greene 261.

'Nowel, nowel, nowel,'
Syng we with myrth.
Cryst is come wel
With vs to dewell
By hys most noble byrth.   5

Vnder a tre in sportyng me
Alone by a wod syd
I hard a mayd that swetly sayd
'I am with chyld this tyd.'
   'Nowell, nowell, nowell,'   10
   Syng we with myrth.
   Cryst is come wel
   With vs to dewell
   By hys most noble byrth.

'Gracyusly conceyuyd haue I   15
The Son of God so swete.
Hys gracyous wyll I put me tyll
As moder hym to kepe.'
   'Novell, novell, novell,'
   Syng we with myrth, etc.   20

19–20. MS novell etc.

'Both nyght and day I wyl hym pray
And her hys lawes taught
And euery dell hys trewe gospell
In hys apostles fraught.'
    'Nowell, nowell, nowell,'   25
    Syng we with myrth, etc.

'Thys goostly case dooth me enbrance
Withowt dyspyt or moke,
With my derlyng lullay to syng
And louely hym to roke.'   30
    'Nowell, nowell, nowell,'
    Syng we with myrth, etc.

'Withowt dystresse in grete lyghtnesse
I am both nyght and day.
This heuenly fod in hys chyldhod   35
Schal dayly with me play.'
    'Nowell, nowell, nowell,'
    Syng we with myrth, etc.

'Soone must I syng with rejoycyng,
For the tym is all rone   40
That I schal chyld all vndefyld
The kyng of Hevens Sonne.'
    'Nowell, nowell, nowell,'
    Syng we with myrth, etc.

93   *Tyrle, Tyrlo*   Later 15 c.

Bodley MS Eng. poet. e. 1, f. 60. Greene 79.

    Tyrle, tyrlo,
    So merylye the shepperdis began to blowe.

41. MS vndefylyt, *then* d *written over second* y
10–14, 25–6, 31–2, 37–8, 43–4. MS nowell etc.

Abowt the fyld thei pyped full right
Even abowt the middis off the nyght.
Adown frome heven thei saw cum a lyght.   5
    Tyrle, tirlo.

Of angels ther came a company
With mery songis and melody.
The shepherdis anonne gane them aspy.
    Tyrle, tirlo.   10

Gloria in excelsis, the angels song
And said who peace was present among
To euery man that to the faith wold long.
    Tyrle, tyrlo.

The shepheris hyed them to Bethleme   15
To se that blyssid sons beme,
And ther they found that glorious streme.
    Tyrle, tyrlo.

Now preye we to that mek chyld
And to his mothere that is so myld,   20
The wich was neuer defyld.
    Tyrle, tyrlo.

That we may cum vnto his blysse,
Where joy shall neuer mysse.
Than may we syng in paradice,   25
    'Tyrle, tirlo.'

I pray yow all that be here
Fore to syng and mak good chere
In the worschip off God thys yere.
    Tyrle, tirlo.   30

94   *Make We Mere As We May*   4 Oct. 1500

This carol is dated by a Latin rubric at the end, stating that it was written on the first Sunday following St. Michael's feast in the Sixteenth year after Henry VII's Conquest of England, that is, after Bosworth Field.

BM MS Addit. 14997, f. 44ᵛ. Index 2343. Greene 10.

> Hay, ay, hay, ay,
> Make we mere as we may.

> Now ys Yole comyn with gentyll chere,
> Of merthe and gomyn he has no pere.
> In euery londe where he comys nere   5
> Is merthe and gomyn, I dar wel say.

> Now ys comyn a messyngere
> Of yore lorde, Ser Nu Yere,
> Byddes vs all be mere here
> And make as mere as we may.   10

> Therefore euery mon that ys here
> Synge a caroll on hys manere.
> Yf he con non we schall hym lere
> So that we be mere allway.

> Whosoeuer makes heve chere   15
> Were he neuer to me dere,
> In a dyche I wolde he were
> To dry hys clothys tyll hyt were day.

> Mende the fyre and make gud chere!
> Fyll the cuppe, ser botelere!   20
> Let euery mon drynke to hys fere!
> Thys endes my caroll with care away.

95   *O Synfull Man, Geve Me Thyn Hert*   Ca. 1492
                    By James Ryman

A 'learned' carol in which, both burden and verses, Christ tells of his life and his Passion, in a supplication to man for his love. *Cf* Poem 96 and its commentary.

Camb. Univ. MS Ee. 1. 12. f. 47ᵛ. Index 1125. Greene 269.

Reuert, reuert, reuert, reuert.
O synfull man, geve me thyn hert.

Haue myende howe I mankyende haue take
Of a pure mayde, man, for thy sake,
That were moost bonde moost fre to make.   5
    O synfull man, geve me thyn hert.

Haue myende, thou synfull creature,
I toke baptyme in thy nature
Fro filthe of synne to make the pure.
    O synfull man, geve me thyn hert.   10

Haue myende, man, how I toke the felde,
Vpon my bak bering my shelde;
For payne ne dethe I wolde not yelde.
    O synfull man, yeve me thyn hert.

Haue myende I was put on the rode   15
And for thy sake shedde my hert blode.
Behold my payne, beholde my moode.
    O synfull man, yeve me thyn hert.

Beholde me, hede, hande, foote and side,
Beholde my woundes fyve so wyde,   20
Beholde the payne that I abyde.
    O synfull man, yeve me thyn hert.

Haue myende, man, how fast I was bounde
For thy sake to a pilloure rounde,
Scorged till my bloode fell to grounde.   25
    O synfull man, yeve me thyn hert.

Haue myende how I in fourme of bred
Haue left my flesshe and blode to wedde

10. MS O synfull man geve etc.
14. MS O synfull man geve me etc.   18. MS O synfull etc.

To make the quyk whenne thou art dedde.
  O synfull man, yeve me thyn hert.   30

Haue myende, man, how I haue the wrought,
How with my bloode I haue the bought
And how to blis I haue the brought.
  O synfull man, yeve me thyn hert.

O synfull man, beholde and see   35
What I haue done and do for the.
Yf thou wilte be in blis with me,
  O synfull man, yeve me thyn hert.

Bothe for my dethe and paynes smert
That I suffred for thy desert   40
I aske no more, man, but thyne hert.
  Reuert, reuert, reuert, reuert.

96   *Min Owine Swet Hart, Com Home Agayne* Ca. 1500

A carol in form and theme like Poem 95, but with a burden, unlike Ryman's learned words, touched by the 'plain style' of popular song. Both poems, by convention, imply the presence of the crucified Christ who speaks, but this piece transforms the image from sculptured figure to living deity, not giving evidence, as Greene argues, of someone's iconoclastic prejudice, but producing a startling dramatic effect of shifting focus.

BM MS Royal 17. B. xliii, f. 184. Index *2086. Greene 270.*

    Com home agayne,
    Com home agayne,
    Min owine swet hart, come home agayne.
    Ye are gone astray
    Owt of youer way,   5
    Therefore com home agayne.

 Mankend I cale wich lyith in frale,

6, 30, 34. MS O synfull man etc.

For loue I mad the free.
To pay the det the prise was gret
From hell that I ranssomed the.   10

Mi blod so red for the was shed,
The prise it ys not smale.
Remembre welle what I the tell
And com whan I the kale. . . .

Therefore refreyne and torne agayne   15
And leve thyne owene intent,
The whiche it is contrare, iwos,
Onto mi commavndment.

Thow standest in dout and sekest about
Where that thow mayst me se.   20
Idovles be set mony for to gyt
Wich ys made of stone and tre.

I am no stoke nor no payncted bloke
Nor mad by no mannes hand,
Bot I am he that shall los the   25
From Satan the phinnes bonde.

97   *Ihesus Woundes Ben Welles of Lif*   Late 15/16 c.

As in Poems 95 and 96 the presence of the Crucifixion is implied, but the
speaker here is another person not Jesus, an observer who urges the reader to
submission and love. Literally, the image is of the crucified Christ seen as a
fountain, from whose wounds flows water with a talismanic power: see
Poem 103.

BM MS Arundel 286, f. 3. Index 1787. Brown XV, 100.

Ihesus woundes so wide
Ben welles of lif to the goode,
Namely the stronde of his syde
That ran ful breme on the rode.

8. MS nad   **15.** MS there re fore   **25.** MS an

Yif thee liste to drinke   5
To fle fro the fendes of helle,
Bowe thou doun to the brinke
And mekely taste of the welle.

98   *A God and Yet a Man*   Late 15/16 c.

A 'witty' poem on the paradoxes of Christian faith.

Bodley MS Rawlinson B. 332, flyleaf. Index 37. Brown XV 120. For date see Brown's Notes.

A god and yet a man?
A mayde and yet a mother?
Witt wonders what witt can
Conceave this or the other.

A god and can he die?   5
A dead man, can he live?
What witt can well replie?
What reason reason give?

Gods truth itselfe doth teach it,
Mans witt senckis too farr vnder   10
By reasons power to reach it.
Beleeve and leave to wonder.

99   *Cest le Myrroure pur lez Iofenes Dames*   15 c.

BM MS Harley 116, f. 128. Index 2136. Brown XV, 152.

Cest le myrroure pur lez Iofenes Dames a regardir aud maytyn pur lour testes bealment adressere.

Maist thou now be glade, with all thi fresshe aray,
On me to loke that wyll dystene thi face.

9. MS God

Cest le myrroure . . . adressere: This is the mirror for the young ladies to look into in the morning in order to make up their faces beautifully.

E

Rew on thyself and all thi synne vprace.
Sone shalte thou flytte and seche another place.
Shorte is thy seson here, thogh thou go gay.   5

O maset wriche, I marke the with my mace.
Lyfte vp thy ieye, beholde now and assay.
Yche loke on me aught to put the in affray.
I wyll not spare the for thou arte my pray.
Take hede and turne fro synne while thou has space.   10

O th'ought wel the hede to this, thaught ye say nay.
My tyme muste nedis comme as I manace.
Be lengthe non lyfe may lepe oute of my lace.
I smyte, I sle, I woll graunte no man grace.
Aryse, awake, amend here while thou may.   15
                                            Explicit.

100   *Deth Is So Hasty*   Late 15/16 c.

Death has come for one who cries to God, 'I'm too young', complaining
that his visitant is unnatural. A brief, possibly incomplete, carol sounding the
theme, widespread through the Plague, of Death's insensateness; he spares the
weary old but not the young, the wretched weak but not the happy strong,
the fools, the sots: with equal disregard he also does the opposite. See Poem 90
and its commentary, and *cf* Boethius, *De Cons. Phil.* I, m. 1, 13–16.

Oxf. Balliol MS 354, f. 210. Index 2511. Greene, 373.

To dy, to dy. What haue I
Offendit, that deth is so hasty?

O marcyfull God, maker of all mankynd,
What menyth dethe in hys mynd
And I so yonge of age?   5
Now deth is vnkynd
For he seyth, 'Man, stop thy wynde.'
Thus he doth rage.

11. wel the hede: MS welthe heele

101   *All Ye That Passe*   15 c.

An inflated version of the widespread *memento mori*, e.g.

> All ye here who pass me by,
> As ye now are so was I,
> As now I am shall ye be.
> Remember me, remember me.

Camb. Trinity Coll. MS. 366, flyleaf. Index *237. Robbins* Sec. XIV-XV, *126.*

All ye that passe be thys holy place,
Both spiritual and temporall of euery degre,
Remembyr yourselfe well duryng tyme and space.
I was as ye are nowe, and as I ye shalbe.
Wherfor I beseche you of your benygnite,   5
For the love of Ihesu and hys mothyr Mare,
For my sowle to say a Pater Noster and an Aue.

102   *Riche Alane the Ballid Man*   15 c.

A 'droll' epitaph, one of a tradition of *facetiae* continuing to our day.
BM MS Harley 665, f. 295. Index *1207. Robbins* Sec. XIV-XV, *124.*

Alanus caluus
Iacet hic sub marmore duro.
Vtrum sit saluus
Non curauit necque curo, etc.

Anglice: 5
Here lyeth vnder this marbyll ston
Riche Alane the ballid man.
Whether he be safe or noght
I recke neuer—for he ne roght.

103   *Medicina pro Morbo Caduco et le Fevr*   15 c.

Poems 103-5 are spells against disease, enemies and thieves, in all of which God and Christ provide a talismanic magic. Exorcism is old in Christianity, is found in Old English verse, and survives in popular 'conjures' against the hex which use the instruments of torture at the Crucifixion, as well as the Five Wounds of Christ. To these were added, with the growth of the Virgin's cult, her Five Joys. Such symbols appear on magic rings (see Joan Evans, *Magical Jewels* [Oxford, 1922], especially pp. 126*ff*), and, together with the figure of Christ and Mary as shield against the Enemy and the magic number five of the Pentangle, on Gawain's talismanic shield in *Sir Gawain and the Green Knight* (see lines 619-65). As late as the 18 c. a votive plaque in an Upper Austrian church shows water from Christ's Five Wounds falling upon a Pentangle. The plaque records a cure of hex and fever.

BM MS Sloane 747, f. 57. Index *3911. Robbins* Sec. XIV-XV, *65.*

> In nomine Patris et Filii et Spiritus Sancti,
> > Amen.
>
> What manere of Ivell thou be
> In Goddis name I coungere the.
> I coungere the with the holy crosse   5
> That Iesus was done on with fors.
> I coniure the with nayles thre
> That Iesus was nayled vpon the tree.
> I coungere the with the crowne of thorne
> That Iesus hede was done with skorne.   10
> I coungere the with the precious blode
> That Iesus shewyd vpon the rode.
> I coungere the with woundes fyve
> That Iesus suffred be his lyve.
> I coungere the with that holy spere   15
> That Longenus to Iesus hert can bere.
> I coungere the neuertheless
> With all the vertues of the masse
> And all the holy prayers of Seynt Dorathe.
> > In nomine Patris et Filii et Spiritus Sancti.   20
> > > Amen.

7. MS conure

Agaynst Thy Enemyes

The Latin verses to Christ and the Two Thieves on the Cross, unrecorded
by Walther's *Initia* and *Sprichwörter*, occur also in the margin next to Poem
105, appropriately to a spell against thieves. See Joan Evans, *Magic Jewels*,
p. 128.

Bodley MS Ashmole 1378, p. 61. Supplement 412.5. *See Black.* Catalogue of the
Ashmole MSS (*1845*), *cols. 1063–4.*

> As thou, Lord, dyddest stope and staye
> For thy chosen peopell the Red Sea,
> The ragyng see waves lacking ther course,
> Tyll they had passed Pharaoos forse;
> And as at Josue his invocation   5
> The son abode ouer Gabaon,
> The mone abode and made hir staye
> In Aialon that valleye;
> And as thy sone Jesus did appease
> The wynd and sea and made them sease   10
> When his disciples with fearefull spryte
> From his sleape ded hym excyte;
> So, Lord of Hostis, staye eche one
> Of those that seake my confusyon.
> Make them stonde as styll as stone   15
> Withowt corporall moving
> Vntyll my stretched arme shall make
> A sygne to them ther way to take;
> As Moses stretched the Red Sea moved
> To show his course as behoved.   20
> As thow, Lord, arte the king of blesse,
> Lord Messyas, grante me this.
> Then saye:
>> *Dismas et Gismas*
>> *Medioque deuina potestas:*   25
>> *Summa petit Dismas,*
>> *Infelix ad infima Gismas.*
>> *Nos et res nostras*
>> *Salvet deuina potestas.*
>>> Finis.

All Theves for to Lett   Late 15/16 c.

See commentary to Poem 104.

Bodley MS Ashmole 1378, f. 77. Index 3771. Robbins Sec. XIV-XV, 63.

To the Holy Goste my goodes I bequeth
That in this place be set,
To the Father and the Sone
All theves for to lett.
And if any theves hyther come   5
My goodys away to fett,
The Holy Goste be them before
And make them for to let,
And make them to abyde
Tyll I agayne come,   10
Thorough the vertu of the Holy Gost,
The Father and the Sonne.

Now I go my way, tyde what may betyd.
If any theves hyther come, here ye shall abyde.
I bynd yow theves   15
And do yow not steare,
So St. Bartylmew bownd the Devyll
With his bearde so hoare. . . .

14. ye: MS I
16. not steare: MS *read with ultra violet lamp:* no. s.are (*Robbins* Sec. XIV, XV, *63, line 16, reads* coniure)
18. Text ends incomplete.

Secular Poems of the Fifteenth Century

I Haue a Newe Garden Earlier 15 c.

Poems 106-8 occur close together in the same MS, begin with the 'I have a' formula and use nursery rhymes for enigma and *double entendre*, The present 'sinful' poem, based on the figure of grafting, plays with *annominatio*, that is, with two words of different meaning which sound alike: the result is not a St. John's pear (a variety of pear ripening early on St. John's day) but one whose *père* is Robert.

BM MS Sloane 2593, f. 11ᵛ. Index 1302. Robbins Sec. XIV-XV, 21.

I haue a newe gardyn
And newe is begunne,
Swych another gardyn
Know I not vnder sunne.

In the myddis of my gardyn   5
Is a peryr set
And it wele non per bern
But a pere Ienet.

The fayrest mayde of this toun
Preyid me   10
For to gryffyn her a gryf
Of myn pery tre.

Quan I hadde hem gryffid
Alle at here wille,
The wyn and the ale   15
Che dede in fille.

And I gryffid here
Ryht vp in here home,

18. home: *emended Robbins* (Sec. XIV, XV, *21*); MS honde

And be that day xx wowkis
It was qwyk in here womb.   20

That day twelfus month
That mayde I mette,
Che seyd it was a pere Robert
But non pere Ionet.

107   *I Haue a Yong Suster*   Earlier 15 c.

A riddling poem connected with love and related to a still surviving nursery
rhyme: see *Oxford Dictionary of Nursery Rhymes*, edited by Opie (1951), 478.
See also Robbins' Note, which suggests connections with popular ballad
themes.

BM MS Sloane 2593, f. 11ʳᵛ. Index 1303. Robbins Sec. XIV-XV, 45.

I haue a yong suster fer beyondin the se.
Many be the drowryis that che sente me.

Che sente me the cherye withoutyn ony ston
And so che ded the dowe withoutyn ony bon.

Sche sente me the brer withoutyn ony rynde,   5
Sche bad me loue my lemman withoute longgyng.

How xuld ony cherye be withoute ston?
And how xuld only dowe ben withoute bon?

How xuld ony brer ben withoute rynde?
How xuld y loue myn lemman without longyng?   10

Quan the cherye was a flour than hadde it no stone.
Quan the dowe was an ey than hadde it non bon.

Quan the brer was onbred than hadde it non rynd.
Quan the maydyn haht that che louit, che is without longing.

24. MS Ion   **4.** the: *supplied*

108   *I Haue a Gentil Cook*   Earlier 15 c.

This elegant account, similar in some respects to that of Chantecleer in Chaucer's *Nun's Priest's Tale*, is related to earlier Latin descriptions of *gallus*, as, e.g., in Alexander Neckam's *De Natura Rerum;* and 'in myn ladyis chaumbyr', also found in nursery rhyme (see Opie's *Dictionary*, 190), has an amatory implication.

BM MS Sloane 2593, f. 10ᵛ. Index *1299. Robbins Sec. XIV-XV, 46.*

I haue a gentil cook, crowyt me the day;
He doth me rysyn erly my matyins for to say.

I haue a gentil cook, comyn he is of gret;
His comb is of reed corel, his tayil is of get.

I haue a gentyl cook, comyn he is of kynde;   5
His comb is of red corel, his tayl is of Inde.

His leggis ben of asour so gentil and so smale,
His sporis arn of syluer qwyt into the wortewale.

His eynyn arn of cristal lokyn al in aumbyr,
And euery nyht he perchit hym in myn ladyis chaumbyr.   10

109   *Kyrieleyson*   Earlier 15 c.

A carol with a play on words (Alison, eleison) from the MS of Poems 106-8. The technique of the narrator, still charmed by her recollection, is that of building up seductive circumstance to a dramatic but not wholly unexpected conclusion.

BM MS Sloane 2593, f. 34. Index *377. Robbins Sec. XIV-XV, 27. Greene 457.*

Kyrie, so Kyrie,
Iankyn syngyt merie
With Aleyson.

108. **1.** the: *supplied*   **6.** MS scorel
    E*

As I went on Yol Day in owre prosessyon,
Knew I ioly Iankyn be his mery ton,   5
Kyrieleyson.

Iankyn began the offys on the Yol Day,
And yyt me thynkyt it dos me good, so merie gan he say,
'Kyrieleyson.'

Iankyn red the pystyl ful fayre and ful wel,   10
And yyt me thinkyt it dos me good as euer haue I sel:
Kyrieleyson.

Iankyn at the Sanctus crakit a merie note,
And yyt me thinkyt it dos me good; I payid for his cote.
Kyrieleyson.   15

Iankyn crakit notis an hunderid on a knot,
And yyt he hakkyt hem smallere than wortis to the pot.
Kyrieleyson.

Iankyn at the Agnus beryt the pax brede.
He twynkelid but sayd nowt, and on myn fot he trede. 20
Kyrieleyson.

Benedicamus domino, Cryst fro schame me schylde.
Deo gracias therto—alas, I go with chylde.
Kyrieleyson.

110   *Man, Bewar of Thin Wowyng*   Earlier 15 c.

A poem against women in the shape of a carol, some lines of which seem popular and proverbial: see Robbins' Notes, and *cf* line 6 ('knet vp the heltre and let here goo') with Robbins 181, lines 16, 32 and 48.

BM MS Sloane 2593, f. 9ᵛ. Index 1938. Robbins Sec. XIV–XV, 41. Greene 403.

Man, bewar of thin wowyng
For weddyng is the longe wo.

6, 12, 15, 21. *supplied*   **23.** chylde: MS schylde   **18, 24.** MS k

Loke er thin herte be set,
Lok thou wowe er thou be knet,
And if thou se thou mow do bet   5
Knet vp the heltre and let here goo.

Wyuys be bothe stowte and bolde,
Her husbondis ayens hem durn not holde,
And if he do his herte is colde
Howsoeuere the game go.   10

Wedowis be wol fals, iwys,
For they cun bothe halse and kys
Til onys purs pikyd is
And they seyn, 'Go, boy, goo.'

Of madenys I wil seyn but lytil   15
For they be bothe fals and fekyl
And vnder the tayl ben ful tekyl.
A twenty deuel name, let hem goo!

111   *An Old Wyf and a Stayle Cvp*   Earlier 15 c.

This piece, of which the first line—here restored by light of lamp and
guess—is erased in the MS, is listed by *Index* and *Supplement* under lines 2
and 5.

*Bodley MS Douce 257, f. 99ᵛ. Index *63 and Supplement *3533.5. Robbins
Sec. XIV-XV, 42.*

An old wyf and a stayle cvp,
Ther ys no merth yn nothir.
A man that hath yteyd hym vp
May nawht chese another.

12. they: *supplied*
1. *Line erased in MS, read with ultra violet lamp:* An old wyf . . . a . . . y.e. cvp;
the rest conjecture

A yong wyf and an arvyst gos,   5
Moche gagil ys with bothe.
A man that hath ham yn his clos
Reste schale he wrothe.

112   *May No Man Slepe in Youre Halle,*   Earlier 15 c.
                        Madame
                        Cantelena

Camb. Univ. MS Addit. 5943, ff. 170ᵛ–171. Index 2135. Robbins Sec. XIV–XV,
31.

May no man slepe in youre halle
For dogges, madame, for dogges, madame,
But yyf he haue a tent of XV ynche
With twey clogges
To dryve awey the dogges, madame.   5
Iblessyd be such clogges
That yyueth such bogges
Bytwyne my lady legges
To dryve awey the dogges, madame.

May no man slepe in youre halle   10
For rattys, madame, for rattys, madame,
But yyf he haue a tent of XV enche
Wyt letheryn knappes
To dryve awey the rattys, madame.
Iblessyd be suche knappes   15
That yyveth such swappes
Vnder my lady lappes
To dryve awey the rattys, madame.

May no man slepe in youre halle
For flyes, madame, for flyes, madame   20

111. **6.** ys *supplied*   112. **5.** to dryve . . . dogges: *supplied*
9. *supplied*   112. **3, 12.** MS ten tent
19. halle: *omitted* MS   **20.** *repetition of* for flyes, madame: *omitted* MS

But yyf he haue a tent of XV enche
Wyt twey byes
To dryve awey the flyes, madame.
Iblessyd be such byes
That maketh such suyes   25
Bytwynne my lady thyes
To dryve awey the flyes madame.

<table>
<tr><td>113</td><td>Our Ser Iohn</td><td>15 c.</td></tr>
</table>

113   *Our Ser Iohn*   15 c.

California Huntington MS EL 1160, f. 11. Index *2494.* Robbins Sec. XIV-XV,
26.

Hey noyney!
I wyll loue our Ser Iohn and I loue eny.

O Lord, so swett Ser Iohn dothe kys
At euery tyme when he wolde pley,
Off hymselfe so plesant he ys   5
I haue no powre to say hym nay.

Ser Iohn loues me and I loue hym,
The more I loue hym the more I maye.
He says, 'Swett hart, cum kys me trym.'
I haue no powre to say hym nay.   10

Ser Iohn to me is proferyng
For hys plesure ryght well to pay,
And in my box he puttes hys offryng.
I haue no powre to say hym nay.

Ser Iohn ys taken in my mouse trappe,   15
Fayne wold I haue hem bothe nyght and day.
He gropith so nyslye abought my lape
I haue no pore to say hym nay.

21-22. yyf . . . twey byes: *omitted* MS   7. loues: MS loue
11. is: MS in

Ser Iohn geuyth me relyus rynges
With praty plesure for to assay,   20
Furres off the fynest with other thynges:
I haue now powre to say hym nay.

114   *Ladd Y the Daunce a Myssomur Day*   Mid 15 c. or before

Cf Poem 109 and its commentary.

Camb. Caius Coll. MS 383, p. 41. Index *1849. Robbins* Sec. XIV-XV, *28.*
Greene 453.

Alas, ales, the wyle,
Thout y on no gyle,
So haue y god chaunce.
Alas, ales, the wyle,
That euer y cowde daunce.   5

Ladd y the daunce a Myssomur Day,
Y made smale trippus, soth for to say.
Iak oure haly watur clerk com be the way
And he lokede me vpon, he thout hit was gay.
Thout yc on no gyle.   10

Iak, oure haly watur clerk, the yonge strippelyng,
For the chesone of me he com to the ryng
And he trippede on my to and made a twynkelyng,
Euer he cam ner, he sparet for no thynge.
Thout y on no gyle.   .15

Iak, ic wot, preyede in my fayre face,
He thout me full worly, so haue y god grace.
As we turndun owre daunce in a narw place
Iak bed me the mouth, a cussynge ther was.
Thout y on no gyle.   20

Iak tho began to rowne in myn ere:
'Loke that thou be priuey and graunte that thou the bere,

8. MS clek   15. no gyle: *supplied*   20. MS no g

A peyre wyth glouus ic ha to thyn were.'
'Gramercy, Iacke,' that was myn answere.
Thoute yc on no gyle.   25

Sone aftur euensong Iak me mette:
'Com hom aftur thy glouus that ic the byhette.'
Wan ic to his chambur com, doun he me sette;
From hym mytte y nat go wan we were mette.
Thout y on no gyle.   30

Schetus and chalonus, ic wot, a were yspredde;
Forsothe tho Iak and yc wenten to bedde.
He prikede and he pransede, nolde he neuer lynne;
Yt was the murgust nyt that euer y cam ynne.
Thout y on no gyle.   35

Wan Iak had don tho he rong the belle.
Al nyht ther he made me to dwelle;
Ofte, y trewe, we haddun yserued the reaggeth deuel of helle;
Of othur smale burdus kep y nout to telle.
Thout y on no gyle.   40

The othur day at prime y come hom, as ic wene;
Meth y my dame coppud and kene:
"Sey, thou stronge strumpeth, ware hastu bene?
Thy trippyng and thy dauncyng wel it wol be sene.'
Thout y on no gyle.   45

Euer bi on and by on my damme reched me clot;
Euer y ber it priuey wyle that y mouth,
Tyl my gurdul aros, my wombe wax out:
'Euel yspunne yern euer it wol out.'
Thout y on no gyle.   50

29. we: *supplied*   **25, 30, 35, 40.** on no gyle: *supplied*

115   *Gracius and Gay*   Mid 15 c. or after

Ireland, Kilkenny Castle MS Ormond, vellum strip. Index 1010. Robbins Sec.
XIV-XV, 143. See St. John D. Seymour, in Proc. Royal Irish Acad. XLI, sec. C
(1932–34), especially pp. 207–8.

> Gracius and gay,
> On hyr lytt all my thohth;
> Butt sche rew on me today,
> To deth sche hatt me broth.
>
> Hyr feyngerys bytt long and small,   5
> Hyr harmus byth rown and toth,
> Hyr mowth as sweth as lycory,
> Vn hyr lyytt all my thoth.
>
> Hyr iyne bytt feyr and gray,
> Hyr bruys bytt well ybenth,   10
> Hyr rode as rede as roose yn May,
> Hyr medyll ys small and gent.
>
> Sche ys swett vnder schett,
> I lowe hyr and no mo.
> Sche hatte myne harth to kepe   15
> In londes wher sche go.
>
> Sodenly tell, y pray,
> To the my low ys lend;
> Kysse me yn my way
> Onys ar y wend.   20

116   *Annys, Annys, Annys, Annys, Annes!*   15 c.

A lover's halleluyah. What a name is Annys!

Bodley MS Douce 381, f. 22. Index 4199. Robbins Sec. XIV-XV, 146. Stainer
I, plate xxiii (facsimile), II, 58–9 (transcription).

> With ryth al my herte now y yow grete,
> With hondert syes, my dere.

8. thoth: MS toth	**11.** Hyr: MS Ass	**14.** and: *supplied*
18. the: *supplied*	**20.** MS wen	

Swete God, yyf vs grace sone to mete
And sone to spekyn yfere.
Annys, Annys, Annys, Annys, Annes!   5
Annes, be now stedfaste on allewys,
And dynke on me, my swete Annys,
My fayre, my sothe Annys.
I love yowre. . . .

117   *Ie Haue So Longe Kepe Schepe on the Grene*   15 c.

Variance in love, the female point of view.

Bodley MS Douce 381, f. 20ᵛ. Index 1312. Robbins Sec. XIV–XV. p. xxxviii.
For music see Stainer I, plate xxi (facsimile), II, 54–5 (transcription).

Ie haue so longe kepe schepe on the grene,
Wilkyne, that alle yowere hert ys sa forhew
So gracius that somme wolde, y wene,
Wilkyne, how that ye wex were vntrew.

Ye may, Wilkyn, wyt rye strawys twyne   5
And pypy as you lyst.
On yowre songe sayth ye loue me best,
Ywys, and moste on yowere thowht.

But that ye seye ye wol for loue dye,
Arys vppon the morne and lust for to pleye.   10
Thys may ryme wel but hyt acorde nouht.

118   *Loue Woll I withoute Eny Variaunce*   15 c.

Bodley MS Ashmole 1393, f. 68ᵛ. Index 2017. Robbins Sec. XIV–XV, 151.
For music, Stainer I, plate xxvi (facsimile), II, 61–2 (transcription).

Loue woll I withoute eny variaunce,
Trewly to serue with all louelynesse,
For yn hit is triste and gentilnesse,
And that may man honour and avaunce.

116. **9.** *Ends imperfectly*   118. **3.** gentilnesse: g *supplied*

119   *Luf Wil I with Variance*   15 c.

Bodley MS Ashmole 191, f. 196ʳ. Index 2016. Robbins Sec. XIV–XV, 152. For music, Stainer I, plate xxxv (facsimile), II, 73–4 (transcriptions).

> Luf wil I with variance
> Because y drede of repentance.
> For whoso loueth withoutyn gouernance,
> Ofttyme it doth hym grevaunce.
> Therfor with avisance   5
> Loue wil I with variaunce.

120   *Go, Hert, Hurt with Aduersite*   15 c.

The love conceit of Heart as servant or messenger which, like the epistle, is sent forth to move and persuade the lady. See Poem 123, and *cf* Poems 89 and 141.

Bodley MS Ashmole 191, f. 192ᵛ. Index 925. Robbins Sec. XIV–XV 155. For music see Stainer I, plate xxxii (facsimile), II, 68–70 (transcription), and hear Argo Record RG 443, item 12.

> Go, hert, hurt with aduersite,
> And let my lady thi woundis see,
> And sey hire this, as y say the:
> Farewel my ioy and welcom peyne
> Til y se my lady agayne.   5

121   *Alas, Fortwne, Thou Art Onkynd*   15 c.

Dublin Trinity Coll. MS 158, f. 92. Index 2245. Robbins Sec. XIV–XV, 158.

> My hert ys so plyngyt yn greffe
> Ther may no barn my balyes onbynd,
> Tyll y onys may sse my leffe
> It wyll not com owt off my mynd.

119. **1, 6.** I: *supplied*   121. **2.** MS bran . . . no byne

Alace, Fortwne, thou art onkynd.   5
Why ssuffrys thou my hart to brek yn two?
For y may not my lady fynd
Y wot y dey for greffe and wo.

122   *Alas, Departynge Ys Ground of Woo*   15 c.

Bodley MS Ashmole 191, f. 195. Index 146. Robbins Sec. XIV-XV, 156. For
music, Stainer I, plate xxxiv (facsimile), II, 72–3 (transcription).

Alas, departynge ys ground of woo.
Other songe can y not synge.
But why part y my lady fro
Syth loue was caus of oure metynge?
The bitter teris of hire wepyng   5
My hert hath pershid so mortaly
That to the deth hit wil me brynge
But yf y se hire hastily.

123   *Go Forth My Hert*   Mid 15 c.

By Charles d'Orléans

A *rondeau* by the French poet, prisoner of the English and in England,
1415–40: see John Fox, *The Lyric Poetry of Charles d'Orléans* (Oxford, 1969).
Following the conventions of the genre, the first two lines are repeated several
times elsewhere in the piece. See Poem 124.

Paris, Bibl. Nat. MS. f. fr. 25458, f. 310. Index 922. Robbins Sec. XIV-XV,
183, and the Notes to 182.

Go forth myn hert wyth my lady,
Loke that ye spar no besynes
To serue hyr wyth seche lowlynes
That ye get hyr grace and mercy.
Pray hyr oftymes pryuely   5
That she quippe trewly hyr promes.

Go forth myn hert wyth my lady,
Loke that ye spar no besynes.
I most as a hertles body
Abyde alone in heuynes,   10
And ye schal dowel wyth your maistres
In plesans glad and mery.

Go forth my hert with my lady.
Loke that ye spar no besynes.

124   *My Gostly Fadir, Y Me Confesse*   Mid 15 c.
                      By Charles d'Orléans

Another *rondeau* by the captive French poet. The glib language, the smooth
verse and the conceit of a penitent confessing a theft and his willingness to
return what was stolen (a kiss) are all marks of a courtly playfulness.

BM MS Harley 682, f. 88ᵛ. Index 2243. Robbins Sec. XIV–XV, *185, and the
Notes to 182.*

My gostly fadir, y me confesse,
First to God and then to yow,
That at a wyndow, wot ye how,
I stale a cosse of gret swetnes,
Which don was out of avisynes.   5
But hit is doon, not vndoon, now.

My gostly fadir, y me confesse,
First to God and then to yow.

But y restore it shall, dowtles,
Ageyn, if so be that y mow;   10
And that to God y make a vow,
And ellis y axe foryefnes.

My gostly fadir, y me confesse,
First to God and then to yow.

123. **7–8, 13–14.** Go . . . besynes: MS Go forth
124. **7, 13.** My . . . confesse: MS My gostly   **11.** to: *supplied*
8, 14. First . . . yow: MS First to

125   *Fortune, Methynk Thou Art Vnkynd*   Mid 15 c.
                    By the Duke of Suffolk

A Complaint against Fortune by the English keeper and host of Charles
d'Orléans, but without the Frenchman's characteristic deftness. It is also like
Poem 121, but without stating that the speaker is fretting for love, a cause
and occasion which courtly convention implies.

*Bodley MS Fairfax 16, f. 321*rv. Index *2567. Robbins* Sec. XIV-XV, *187*.

    A thou Fortune, whyche hast the gouernance
    Of alle thyngys kyndly mevyng to and fro
    Thaym to demene aftyr thyn ordynaunce
    Ryght as thou lyst to graunt hem wele or wo,
    Syth that thou lyst that I be on of tho   5
    That must be reulyd by thyn avysinesse,
    Why wyltow not wythstand myn heuynesse?

    Methynk thou art vnkynd, as in this case,
    To suffre me so long a while endure
    So gret a payn wythout mersy or grase,   10
    Which greuyd me ryght sore, I the ensure.
    And syth thou knowst I am that creature
    That wold be fauoured by thy gentyllesse,
    Why wyltow not wythstonde myn heuynesse?

    What causyth the to be myn aduersarye?   15
    I haue not done that which shulde dysplese,
    And yit thou art to myn entent contrarye,
    Which makyth now sorous to encres.
    And syth thou wost myn hert ys not in ese
    But euer in trouble wythout sykernesse,   20
    Why wyltow not wythstande myn heuynesse?

    To the allonly this compleynt I make,
    For thou art cause of myn aduersyte,

16. MS whiche that

And yit I wot wele thou mayst vndirtake
For myn welfare yf that thou lyst agre.   25
I haue no cause to blame no wyght but the,
For thys thou doost of very wylfulnesse.
Why wyltow not wythstand myn heuynesse?

126   *Myn Hertys Ioy*   Mid 15c.
                  By the Duke of Suffolk

Bodley MS Fairfax 16, ff. 323ᵛ–324. Index *2182.* Robbins *Sec.* XIV-XV, *189.*
Cf. Index *2247.*

Myn hertys ioy and all myn hole plesaunce,
Whom that I serue and shall do faythfully
Wyth trew entent and humble obseruance
Yow for to plese in that I can treuly,
Besechyng yow thys lytell byll and I   5
May hertly, wyth symplesse and drede,
Be recomawndyd to your goodlyhede:

And yf ye lyst haue knowlech of my qwert,
I am in hele (God thankyd mot he be)
As of body, but treuly not in hert,   10
Nor nought shal be to tyme I may you se;
But thynke that I as treuly wyll be he
That for your ese shall do my payn and myght
As thogh that I were dayly in your syght.

I wryte to yow no more for lak of space   15
But I beseche the only Trinite
Yow kepe and saue be support of hys grace
And be your sheld from al aduersyte.
Go lytill byll and say thou were wyth me
Of verey trouth, as thou canst wele remembre,   20
At myn vpryst, the fyft day of Decembre.

127   *Swarte Smekyd Smethes*   Mid 15 c.

A *tour de force* of description, in which the heavy artificialities of the alliterative style are made to serve the clangour of the occasion. *Cf* Poems 45 and 144.
BM MS Arundel 292, f. 71ᵛ. Index 3227. Robbins Sec. XIV-XV, 118.

Swarte smekyd smethes smateryd wyth smoke
Dryue me to deth wyth den of here dyntes.
Swech noys on nyghtys ne herd men neuer:
What knauene cry and clateryng of knockes!
The cammede kongons cryen after 'Col, col!'   5
And blowen here bellewys that al here brayn brestes.
'Huf, puf,' seyth that on, 'Haf, paf,' that other.
Thei spyttyn and spraulyn and spellyn many spelles,
Thei gnauen and gnacchen, thei gronys togydere,
And holdyn hem hote wyth here hard hamers.   10
Of a bole hyde ben here barm fellys,
Her schankes ben schakeled for the fere flunderys.
Heuy hamerys thei han that hard ben handled,
Stark strokes thei stryken on a stelyd stokke.
'Lus, bus, las, das,' rowtyn be rowe.   15
Sweche dolful a dreme the Deuyl it todryue!
The mayster longith a lityl and lascheth a lesse,
Twyneth hem tweyn and toucheth a treble:
'Tik, tak, hic, hac, tiket, taket, tyk tak,
Lus, bus, lus, das.' Swych lyf thei ledyn,   20
Alle clothemerys, Cryst hem gyue sorwe!
May no man for brenwaterys on nyght han hys rest.

5. 'The twist-beaked bastards bellow after "Coals, coals!"'
8. *spellyn many spelles:* 'give out many oaths or imprecations' (?)
17-18. 'The master smith lengthens one piece a little and hammers another smaller, then twists them both together and strikes a treble note.' (?) (But *cf* Sisam, *XIV C. Verse and Prose*, pp. 169–70, lines 17–18.)
21. *clothemerys:* 'mare clothers', i.e. horse tailors, i.e. blacksmiths
22. brenwaterys: 'water burners', i.e. blacksmiths (because they plunge hot iron into water, which dissolves into steam)

128   *Thirti Dayes Hath Nouembir*   15 c.

BM MS Harley 2341, f. 5. Index *3571. Robbins* Sec. XIV-XV, *68.*

> Thirti dayes hath Nouembir,
> April, Iune and Septembir;
> Of eight and twenti is but oon,
> And all the remenaunt thirti and oon.

129   *Wytte Is Trechery*   15 c.

Bodley MS Ashmole 750, f. 100ᵛ. Index *906. For variants see Brown* XV, *175
and Notes. For Latin, Walther,* Sprichwörter, *12366.*

> *Ingenium dolus est, amor omnis voluptas,*
> *Ludus rusticitas et gula festa dies;*
> *Senex ridetur, mulier pulsat amore,*
> *Diues laudatur, pauper adheret humo;*
> *Prudentes ceci, cognati degeneres sunt,*   5
> *Mortuus ignotus, nullus amicus erit.*

> Wytte is trechery, loue is lechery,
> Play is vileney and holyday is glotony;
> Olde man is skorned, yong woman is wowed,
> Ryche man is glosed and poure man is bowed;   10
> Sleght men been blynde and kyn ben vnkynde,
> The deed is out of mynde and frend may no man fynde.

130   *Hedles, Hanles, Movthles, Legles*   Late 15 c.

A Latin text occurs in Bodley MS Rawlinson D. 328, f. 144, with the first
two lines of the English:

> Tres homines assifoli ad pilam ludebant;
> Vnus homo mancus hiis omnibus seruebat

6. MS *omitted; cf Brown* XV, *Notes to 175*

Dum hori carens stabat et ridebat
Et unus decrepitus mantellum tradebat.

Bodley MS Eng. Poet. e. 1, f. 26ᵛ. Index *1354. Robbins* Sec. XIV-XV, *Notes to 45.*

I saw thre hedles playen at a ball;
On hanles man served hem all;
Whyll thre movthles men lay and low
Thre legles away hem drow.

131   *Her I Was and Her I Drank*   15 c.

Dublin Trinity Coll. **214**, *f. 1.* Index *1201. Robbins* Sec. XIV-XV, *12.*

Her I was and her I drank,
Farwyll, dam, and mykyll thank.
Hcr I was and had gud cher
And her I drank wyll gud ber.

132   *The Boris Hede in Hond I Bryng*   Late 15 c.

The first three stanzas of this carol are like the entire carol in Oxford Balliol Coll. MS 354, f. 228, but are here given as for the first course in an elaborate meal, described in the subsequent stanzas. The whole development is by listing and naming.

MS Porkington 10, f. 202. Index *3314. Robbins* Sec. XIV-XV, *56. Greene 135. See also Robbins 53-55 and their Notes, and Greene 132-34 and their Notes.*

Hey, hey, hey, hey!
The borrys hede is armyd gay.

The boris hede in hond I bryng
Witt garlond gay in porttoryng.
I pray yow all witt me to synge,   5
Witt hay!

131. **3.** Her: MS he

Lordys, knyghttus and skyers,
Persons, prystis and wycars,
The boris hede ys the furst mes,
Witt hay!   10

The boris hede, as I yow say,
He takis his leyfe and goth his way
Son after the Tweylffyt Day,
Witt hay!

Then commys in the secund kowrs witt mykyll pryid: 15
The crannus and the heyrrons, the bytteris by ther syde,
The pertrychys and the plowers, the wodcokus and snyt,
Witt hay!

Larkys in hot schow, ladys for to pyk,
Good drynk therto, lycyvs and fyn: 20
Blwet of allmayn, romnay and wyin,
        Witt hay!

Gud bred, alle and wyin, dare I well say,
The boris hede witt musterd armyd soo gay,

Furmante to potdtage witt wennissun fyn   25
And the hombuls of the dow and all that euer commis in,

Capons ibake witt the pesys of the roow,
Reysons of corrans witt odyr spysis moo.

---

133   *Bryng Vs in Good Ale*   Late 15 c.

A carol which is also a drinking song, proceeding by a series of negative *distinctiones*.

Bodley MS Poet. e. 1, ff. 41ᵛ–42. Index 549. Robbins Sec. XIV–XV, 13. Greene 422A.

Bryng vs in good ale and bryng vs in good ale,
Fore owr Blyssyd Lady sak, bring vs in good ale.

9. MS furt   **13.** Tweylffyt: MS XII theylffyt   **18.** MS ha

Bryng vs in no browne bred fore that is mad of brane,
Nor bryng vs in no whyt bred fore therin is no game,
But bryng vs in good ale.   5

Bryng vs in no befe for ther is many bonys,
But bryng vs in good ale for that goth downe at onys,
And bryng vs in good ale.

Bryng vs in no bacon for that is passyng fate,
But bryng vs in god ale and gyfe vs inought of that,   10
And bryng vs in good ale.

Bryng vs in no mutton for that is often lene,
Nor bryng vs in no trypys for thei be syldom clene,
But bryng vs in good ale.

Bryng vs in no eggys for ther ar many schellys,   15
But bryng vs in good ale and gyfe vs nothing ellys,
And bryng vs in good ale.

Bryng vs in no butter for therin ar many herys,
Nor bryng vs in no pyggys flesch for that wyl mak vs borys,
But bryng vs in good ale.   20

Bryng vs in no podyngys for therin is al gotys blod,
Nor bryng vs in no veneson for that is not for our good,
But bryng vs in good ale.

Bryng vs in no capons flesch for that is often der,
Nor bryng vs in no dokys flesch for thei slober in the mer,   25
But bryng vs in good ale.

| 134 | *Fill the Boll, Ientill Butler* | Late 15/16 c. |

Another drinking carol, with the speaker of the verses slightly tight and not
above a simple pun (line 23—Water, Walter).

Oxf. Balliol Coll. MS 354, ff. 251ᵛ–252. Index *903. Robbins* Sec. XIV–XV, *14.*
Greene 421.

21. MS godys good   **22.** good: MS blod

How, butler, how! Bevis à towt!
Fill the boll, ientill butler, and let the cup rowght!

Ientill butler, bell amy,
Fyll the boll by the eye
That we may drynk by and by.   5
    With how, butler, how! Bevis à towt!
    Fill the boll, butler, and let the cup rowght!

Here is mete for vs all,
Both for gret and for small.
I trow we must the butlar call.   10
    With how, butler, how! Bevis à towght!
    Fill the boll, butler, and lett the cupe rowght!

I am so dry I cannot spek,
I am nygh choked with my mete.
I trow the butler be aslepe.   15
    With how, butler, how! Bevis à towght!
    Fill the boll, butler, and let the cup rowght!

Butler, butler, fill the boll
Or ellis I beshrewe thy noll!
I trow we must the bell toll.   20
    With how, butler, how! Bevis à towght!
    Fill the boll, butler, and let the cup rowght!

Iff the butlers name be Water
I wold he were a galow claper
But if he bryng vs drynk the rather.   25
    With how, butler, how! Bevis à towght!
    Fill the boll, butler, and let the cup rowght!
       Explicit.

1. MS butlet   17. and . . . rowght!: *supplied*
22. butler . . . rowght!: *supplied*   27. the boll . . . rowght!: *supplied*

1. *Bevis à towt:* 'Drinks for all'

135 *Alone Walkyng, In Thought Pleynyng* Late 15 c.

A lover's Complaint, the action of which is the sorrowing thought of a solitary walker: its charm the short lines, frequent rhymes, and the rhyming connection between its stanzas, characteristic of the virelay. The poem is headed 'Chaucer' in the MS.

Camb. Trinity Coll. MS 599 (R.3.19), f. 160. Index *267.* Robbins Sec. XIV-XV, *173.*

Alone walkyng,
In thought pleynyng
And sore syghyng,
All desolate,
Me remembryng 5
Of my lyuyng,
My deth wyssyng
Bothe erly and late,

Infortunate
Ys soo my fate 10
That, wote ye whate,
Oute of mesure
My lyfe I hate.
Thus desperate,
In suche pore estate 15
Do I endure.

Of other cure
Am I nat sure,
Thus to endure
Ys hard, certain. 20
Suche ys my ure,
I yow ensure;
What creature
May haue more payn?

My trouth so pleyn 25
Ys take in veyn

And gret disdeyn
In remembraunce.
Yet I full feyne
Wold me compleyne   30
Me to absteyne
From thys penaunce.

But in substaunce
Noon allegeaunce
Of my greuance   35
Can I nat fynde.
Ryght so my chaunce
With displesaunce
Doth me auaunce—
And thus an ende.   40
    Explicit.

136   *I Must Go Walke the Woed So Wyld*   End 15 c.

Another solitary walker, self-banished because of a lady's deceit to the woods,
which were long the exile's *locus* for sorrowing love: see Poem 18. Robbins
considers this a carol with the burden lacking.

Calif. Huntingdon MS EL 1160, f. 11ᵛ. Index *1333.* Robbins Sec. XIV-XV, *20.*

I must go walke the woed so wyld
And wander here and there
In dred and dedly fere,
For where I trusted I am begyld,
And all for on.   5

Thus am I banysshyd from my blis
By craft and false pretens,
Faultles, without offens,
As off return no certen ys,
And all for fer off on.   10

My bed schall be under the grenwod tre,

A tufft off brakes vnder my hed,
As on from ioye were fled.
Thus from my lyff day by day I flee,
And all for one.   15

The ronnyng stremes shall be my drynke,
Acorns schalbe my fode.
Nothyng may do me good
But when of your bewty I do thynk,
And all for lowe off on.   20

137   *Whane Nettuls in Wynter*   Late 15 c.

An anti-feminist song in rime royal, found also in Balliol Coll. MS 354, f.
250ᵛ, but here lengthened from four to seven stanzas and transformed into a
carol by addition of a burden. As in the drinking carol *Bryng Vs In Good Ale*
(Poem 133), development is by *distinctiones*, in the present case a list of *im-
possibilia* from nature. This last figure, called *adynata* by the rhetoricians, appears
frequently in medieval satire: see E. R. Curtius, *European Literature and the
Latin M.A.*, translated by Trask (New York, 1953), pp. 94–8. *Cf Cambridge
M.E. Lyrics*, edited by Person (Seattle, 1962), 50, which adds a Latin apophthegm
on a woman's renouncing tears, also impossible in nature: *Didiscere flere* =
Publilius Syrus, edited by Friedrich (1880), p. 38.

Bodley MS Eng. Poet. e. 1, ff. 43ᵛ–45. Index *3999. Greene 402A. Cf Robbins* Sec.
XIV–XV, *114*.

Whane thes thyngys foloyng be done to our intent
Than put women in trust and confydent.

When nettuls in wynter bryng forth rosys red
And al maner of thorn trys ber fygys naturally
And ges ber perles in euery med   5
And laurell ber cherys abundantly
And okys ber datys very plentuosly
And kyskys gyfe of hony superfluens,
    Than put women in trust and confydens.

19. of: supplied.   thynk: MS thyn

Whan box ber papur in euery lond and towne   10
And thystuls ber berys in euery place
And pykys have naturally fethers in ther crowne
And bullys of the see syng a good bace
And men be the schypys fyschys do trace
And in women be fownd no incypyens,   15
      Than put hem in trust and confydens.

Whan whytyngys do walke forestys to chase herrtys
And heryngys ther hornnys in forestys boldly blow
And marmsattys morn in morys and in lakys
And gurnardys schot rokys owt of a crosebow   20
And goslyngys hunt, the wolfe to ouerthrow
And spratys ber sperys in armys of defens,
      Than put women in trust and confydens.

Whan swyn be conyng in al poyntys of musyke
And assys be docturs of euery scyens   25
And kattys do hel men be practysyng of fysyke
And boserds to Scryptur gyfe ony credens
And marchans by with horne insted of grotys and pens
And pyys be mad poetys for ther eloquens,
      Than put women in trust and confydens.   30

Whan spawyns byld chyrchys on a hyth
And wrenys cary sekkys onto the myll
And curlews cary tymber, howsys to dyth
And semavs ber butter to market to sell
And wodkokys wer wodknyfys, cranis to kyll   35
And gren fynchys to goslyngys do obedyens,
      Than put women in trust and confydens.

Whan crowbys tak sarmon in wodys and parkys
And be tak with swyftys and snaylys
And cammels in the ayer tak swalows and larkys   40
And myse move movntans with wagyng of her taylys
And schypmen tak a ryd insted of saylles
And whan wyfvys to her husbondys do no offens,
      Than put women in trust and confydens.

Whan hantlopys sermovntys eglys in flyght   45
And swans be swyfter than haukys of the tower
And wrennys ses goshaukys be fors and myght
And musketys mak vergese of crabbys sower
And schyppys seyl on dry lond, sylt gyfe flower
And apys in Westmynstur gyfe jugment and sentens,   50
    Than put women in trust and confydens.

138   *For to Praysse This Praty Woman*   Late 15 c.

A carol against women in the form of a series of 'comparisons', which also
appear, with additions, in a 15 c. cypher: see *A Common-Place Book of the
Fifteenth Century* edited by L. T. Smith (London, 1886), pp. 12–13.
*Bodley MS Eng. Poet. e. 1, f.13*rv. Index *3552*. Wright Carols and Songs (*Percy
Soc., XXIII*), iv.

        Herfor and therfor and therfor I came
        And for to praysse this praty woman.

    Ther wer thre wylly, thre wyly ther wer:
    A fox, a fryyr and a woman.
        Herfor and therfor and therfor I came   5
        And for to praysse this praty woman.

    Ther wer thre angry, thre angry ther wer:
    A wasp, a wesyll and a woman.
        Herfor and therfor and therfor I came
        And for to praysse this praty woman.   10

    Ther wer thre cheteryng, thre cheteryng ther wer;
    A peye, a jaye and a woman.
        Herfor and therfor and therfor I came
        And for to praysse this praty woman.

    Ther wer thre wold be betyn, thre wold be betyn ther wer: 15
        A myllston, a stocke fysche and a woman.
        Herfor and therfor and therfor I came
        And for to praysse this praty woman.

29, 35, 50. MS eloques, wodkyfys, sentes
5–6, 9–10, 13–14, 17–18. supplied
    F

The attribution to Chaucer looks to us like a Scots scribe's joke, but medieval readers had, on the whole, remarkably little sense of an author's canon.

Nat. Lib. Scotland MS Advocates 1.1.6, f. 263. Index *2580. Robbins* Sec. XIV-XV, 212.

O wicket wemen, wilfull and variable,
Richt fals, feckle, fell and frivolus,
Dowgit, dispytfull, dour and dissavable,
Vnkynd, crewall, curst and covettus,
Ouirlicht of laitis, vnleill and licherus,   5
Turnit fra trewth and taiclit with treichery,
Vnferme of faith, fulfillit of fellony!

O stowt, stif, standfra and vnstable,
Vnmeik but mesur and malitius,
Angry, awstern and till all evillis able,   10
Skornand, skaithful, skald and most sklandrus,
Gredy, not gude, grym, gray and vngratius,
Noyus but neid and full of iniquitie,
Vngentill, iugeit and full of iolesie!

Als terne as tygir, of tung vntollerable,   15
O thow violent virago vennemouss!
Blasterand, bald, brym and abhominable,
Ourperte, reprevivable, peirles and perrellous,
Evil Christiane, vnknawin, crafty and cawtelus,
Vnchest, evill chosin and all but cheretie,   20
Mellit with misdeid and all mensworne are ye!
    Finis quod Chauceir

Camb. U. MS. Ff. 1.6., f. 56. Index *3917. Robbins, 'The Findern Anthology',* PMLA *LXIX (1954), p. 632.*

What so men seyn,
Loue is no peyn
To them, serteyn,

Butt varians.
For they constreyn   5
Ther hertis to feyn,
Ther mowthis to pleyn
Ther displeasauns.

Whych is indede
Butt feynyd drede,   10
So God me spede,
And dowbilnys:
Ther othis to bede,
Ther lyuys to lede,
And proferith mede   15
Newfangellnys.

For when they pray
Ye shall haue nay,
What so they sey
Be ware for shame.   20
For euery daye
They waite ther pray
Wherso they may
And make butt game.

Then semyth me   25
Ye may well se
They be so fre
In eyery plase,
Hitt were pete
But they shold be   30
Begelid, parde,
Withowtyn grase.

141   *Sho Se Me in a Kirk on a*   Early 16 c.
                 Friday in a Mornyng

The poetic Epistle common to amatory tradition and to the 15 c., but un-
common for its reality, for the uneven movement of its lines, and for the charm

of its whimsical detail: *cf* Poem 109. It is from the Commonplace Book of Humfrey Newton together with Poems 142 and 143, all of which bring to conventional formulas a similar realistic particularity as they chronicle the start and hapless end of an adventure in 'true' love. *Cf* the one realistic touch, the date line, in the lover's 'Lettyr' of Poem 126.

Bodley MS Lat. Misc. C. 66, f. 94, col. 2. Index 926. Robbins Sec. XIV-XV, 194, and cf PMLA LXV (1950) p. 271, item xiv.

Go, litull bill, and command me hertely
Vnto her that I call my trulof and lady,
Be this same tru tokynnynge
That sho se me in a kirk on a Friday in a mornyng
With a sperhauk on my hand,   5
And my mone did by her stond.
And an old womon sete her by
That litull cold of curtesy,
And oft on her her sho did smile
To loke on me for a wile.   10
And yet be this another token,
To the kirk sho comme with a gentilwomen.
Euen behynd the kirke dore
They kneled bothe on the flore
And fast thay did pitur-patur: 15
I hope thay said matens togeder!
Yet ones or twyes, at the lest,
Sho did on me her ee kest.
Then went I forthe preuely
And haylsed on thaym curtesly.   20
Be alle the tokens truly
Command me to her hertely.

142   *By God of Loue Set I Nothyng*   Early 16 c.

   The narrative of a scorner's captivation in rhyming stanzas of eight lines of uneven length, and notable, like Poem 141, for its cursive realism. For a similar

9. *on her her:* at her in this (i.e. my) direction'

story see the fall of the scorner Troilus in Chaucer's *Troilus and Criseyde*. The
state of the lines (see the textual notes) suggests a poem in revision.

Bodley MS Lat. Misc. C. 66, ff. 93, left margin—93ᵛ, left and top margins. Index
572. Robbins, PMLA LXV, pp. 264–6, item vi.

By god of loue set I nothyng
Nor by Venus with her vaynglorie I wold not aply,
For I thoght playnly, al in my hethyng,
There wos no women ynder God that shuld make me sore,
Ne non that I wold loue bot a seson and a while,   5
Thof sho were neuer so feire and fresh of face;
For I trustid hem not, I said they wold me begele
And hynge me in her bondon and then gruche me her grace.

Bot nowe is Venus wroth at my veyn wordis
And has send out her meyden me for to tene,   10
To dele me a darte of loue as sharp as any swordis
And haue bitturly me bonden in loue chene.
And how she keht me with croke for to loue a mey
I shall telle yo titely and wond for no blame:
To the kirk I went ones on a holy day   15
To here mes, for sothe, all togeder in same.

I was avised on a wegh that did by me knelle,
Late commyn fro court ale her for to play,
And then Venus was set deftnes to dele
And garte me to kest my ee on that faire mey,   20
And sho with broes brent and een that were gray
To me anon sho kest her sight.
Then loued I lely, this is no nay,
And my hert in hers anon hit was plight.

Bot yet I wist not, for sothe, what that brude thoht,   25
Wheder I was a wegh naht to here pay.

3. MS thoh   9. MS vey   11. MS a sharp
23. *Between* I *and* lely: MS h *crossed out and* holly *inserted below* this is
25. what . . . thoht: MS what that she thoht, *and* brud *written above* she thoht
26. naht: MS na

Herk now or after and ye shall well se
How it happene anon after on another day.
I was in felischip with her on Witsontyme
And broht her a myle onward on the way.   30
And then to my purpas sho did incline
And said sho had no luf and swere by thys day.

And then I speke spakly and spered her anon
And sed I was lufsek euen for her sak.
And she cald me a scorner and sage and said I was won.   35
And then to her mercy I did me betak.
Then I prayd her for pete if that scho wold
Ones on haly abras me for my seke,
Or ellis my cares thay wold wax more cold
And my blis, thus canseled, she myht abate.   40

She said de she wold indeid for my sake
Bot wheder she myht or not she cold not wel telle me.
I said a tokyn sho most vnto me take.
Sho said the right hond glofe shuld it be.
'And if the lift be of, then may ye se   45
That ye may not cum nether erly ne lat.
This is the tokyn, thus let it bee.
Ye may se now what I do euen for youre sake.'

Then met I that may that was bright and shen
And kest her and klepped her at my wele.   50
She said she loued me and that myght I sen,
And I said she myht me lith saue and spil.
She bid me pittis preues what I welle
And that she loues me lelly with all her hert.

29. MS w. . . . tyme (*dotted space undecipherable*)   30. MS my
31. MS incli (*the rest torn away*)   33. MS & non
50. my wele: MS my wele euen by her lefe; by her *struck out and everything
after* wele *evidently a false start*
51. MS se

35. *sage*: 'jokester'. French 'fol sage', a court jester

She said she will met me in place wher I wold   55
Me to comfort of my care and me to ioy conuerte.

Bot I haue not beddyn that burd mete me in no place
Wher I myhte opyn my hert and say what I wel
My bone for to aske and sho to gront grace,
For I trist in her that she will not me spill.   60
'I haue not,' she said, 'nas neuer nay,
Bot as preues so shall I write.'
Bot and sho do I de this die
And of my dethe sho is the wite.

143   *Alas, a Thousand Sith Alas*   Early 16 c.

The poetic Farewell, in character like Poem 142, of a lover exiled by false
rumours. *Cf* Poem 90 and especially Robbins *Sec. XIV-XV*, 204, in which
there is some of the language ('I take my leve agaynst my wyll') but none of
the particularity.

Bodley MS Lat. Misc. C. 66, f. 94ᵛ, cols. 1 and 3. Index *137. Robbins* PMLA
LXV, pp. 272-4, item xvi.

> Alas, a thousand sith alas,
> For won that is of ble so briht
> That alle my hert for euer sho has
> To haue and hold as I her het.
> Alas, I may not with her speak   5
> That is so faire and fresch of face.
> Alas, how shuld my hert be liht,
> Alas, a thousand sithe alas.
>
> Bot fare wele my rihtwise ioy and blis,
> Fare wele my worschipe and my wele,   10
> Fare wele my myrth withoutyn myse,

55. me: MS e
56. comfort . . . conuerte: MS comfor of my care and my balis lese (e *written
above second* my *and* balis lese *struck through*) to ioy conuerte

---

61. *I have not:* 'I have not caused anyone to die' (?)

Fare wele comfort of home and hele;
Bot fare wele truest and most lelle,
Fare wele as swet as ros on hill,
Fare welle as oft as tong can tell: 15
I take my leue ageyne my will.

Now fare wele the tokens all bedene:
Fare wele the hrynge god and true,
Fare wele bocles, broch so fyne,
Fare wele the rynge of siluer newe.   20
Fare wele the baw bond and the arow therein,
Fare wele the perle so shene,
Fare wele the frends that were with me:
In hast I will cum home agayn.

Now fare well aples faire and swete,   25
Fare wele pomegarnet that was red,
Fare wele the poynt of yelo silk:
Fare wele the lettul wordes that chastyn my mod,
Fare wele the lawes and lettres couert,
Fare wele the berrer tru to layn,   30
Fare wele the reder, and herken most of alle,
For in hast I wil cum home agayn.

Now fare wele the Sondays that we se,
Fare wele the Wennysdays that rull so fast,
Fare wele the sterres appon the sky   35
That nyht I slepe and tak goode rest;
Fare wele the armes that were so fayre,
Fare wele the hond in hond I wene.
To de for her sak me had leuer
Then fro her euer that I wold twyne.   40

But fare wele quene that I loue best

21. MS there im   **22.** shene: *conjecture,* MS *undecipherable*
23. MS fends   **26.** MS *omits* wele
28. MS are wele the lett . . l [*or d*]   **30, 33, 34.** MS fare w
32. MS *omits* agayn   **33.** we *coniecture*   **36.** MS goode & rest

And violet that sho weres on.
How that I fare, wele mot sho rest,
And gif her grace me to thynk on.
Fare wele the kirk that sho did in kneled   45
Bot and the peler mad of ston.
Ther oft on me has she smylid
Bot talis haue fersed me out of ton.

Bot now fare wele lokynge and lahynge bothe,
And fare wele skynnynge on iche sid,   50
To go fro her then am I lothe
So that fals talis I may not abide.
Fare wele, fare wele a thousand sithe.
Be this same tru tokynynge
I tellid you how longe I wold abid.   55
Ye said, alas, how shall I do so longe?

144   *Wyntre Is Gurde Oute and Gon*   Early 16 c.

A spring song beginning with a seasonal poetry commonplace, the turn from
winter to spring, and developing into an invitation to a tumble in the grass.
In the MS these lines are preceded by four similar quatrains describing a castle
on a cliff, the whole appearing to be an elaborate exercise in manner reminiscent
of *Sir Gawain and the Green Knight* and other courtly poetry of its time.

The castle quatrains do not seem to belong with the rest, but if they do the
piece becomes a kind of playful version of a scene from the subject, *The
Labours of the Months*, frequently found in contemporary illumination; in the
famous *Très Riches Heures* of Jean Duc de Berry, month by month, castle forms
background for the appropriate human labours in the foreground—in this
case the 'labours' for April (an out-of-doors betrothal).

The writer's technical ingenuity is demonstrated, not only by alliteration
and the special vocabulary it requires, but also by use of a single pair of rhymes
throughout, with a new pair coming at the end.

From the Commonplace Book of Humfrey Newton.

*Bodley MS Lat. Misc. C. 66, f. 106ᵛ. Index 2682. Robbins. PMLA LXV, pp.
277–9, item xxii.*

45. MS *omits* wele
F*

Wyntre that snartely snewes
And snappes vs with mony snartte snawes
Is gurde oute and gon with her gewes
That mony gome be gloponed with glawes.

The swete somer seyson that sewes,   5
Miche salace to the segges hit sawes.
To herken the hunt howe he hewes
And halows his houndes with hawes.

The brome and the blossum it blewes,
So blithe is the breth that her blawes.   10
The likynge of louers it lewes
That listen to layke by the lawes.

Rise vp without any rewes,
Arayke downe radly by the rawes
And stele to thi steyuen by stewes   15
In strynd or in stide ther it stawes.

And mete with that mayden in mewes
And medell with that meeke with her mawes.
Let her not forthrast the with threwes,
With her threpe ne bethilge the with thawes.   20

For at that tyme if ho tas treweesse
And taries the till eft with her trawes,
Ho will forcast the with her knewes
And come no more to clayme, as thow knows.

Therfore that birde if thou bewes   25
And buxumly in thi armes thou bawes,
Leese not the whene thof ho whewes
With a whip, hey and war now! thof ho whawes.

And thof ho thries threte the thewes
Ne be ho neuer so throe with hir thrawes,   30
Kleche her euen vpt to thi klewes
For a koyntise while ho ther bak klowes.

For while somer foles synges
Loue spreydes and sprynges
And iche man mynges   35
To medel his mak to
And to teche hir that connot for to tak to.

37. *teche* . . . *tak to:* 'teach her who does not know (about love) to marry'

Glossary

i and y *vocalic are alphabetized together, initially and internally, under* i; sc, sch *and* sh *under* sh; u *and* v *vocalic under* u; u *and* v *consonantal under* v; i *and* y *consonantal under* y.

a *interj* ah, o, 55.1
a *pron. 3 sg. fem. see* **hoe**
a *prep. see* **on**
a *vb. see* **hauen**
abyde *vb.* await, 27.8
abras *vb.* embrace, 142.38
abuggen *vb.* pay the penalty, 29.19
ac *conj.* but, 12.28
adreynt *vb. pp.* drowned, 26.23
affy *vb.* trust, 47.32
affray *sb.* fear, 99.8
aght *sb.* aught, 46.37
alesen *vb.* deliver, 10.20
algate *adv.* in any case, 90.9
aliues *adv.* alive 33.4
allegeaunce *sb.* alleviation, 135.34
alute *vb. pret. 3 sg.* = **alihte** descended, 12.22
an *conj.* and, 41.44
an *prep. see* **on**
and *conj.* if, 47.41
aply *vb.* devote oneself, 142.1
arayke *vb. imp. sg.* wander, 144.14
are *adv. see* **her**
areride *vb. pp.* raised up, 16.15
arst *adv.* first, 12.28
arvyst *sb.* harvest, 111.5
aseth *sb.* reparation, 90.5
asteye *vb. pret. 2 sg.* ascended, 10.9
astunde *adv.* for some time, 12.14
ato *adv.* in two, 42.2
avisaunce *sb.* consideration, 119.5
avised (on) *vb.* (was) aware of, 142.17
avisynes *sb.* design, 124.5
aweden *vb.* go mad, 3.38
awelde *vb.* control, 47.52
awreke *vb. pp.* avenged, 73.9
awstern *adj.* harsh, 139.10
ayen *prep.* against, 1.60; **ayens** 110.8

bable *sb.* bauble, 90.24
bahit = **bade** *see* **bidden**
bale *sb.* pain, 33.34; *pl.* **balus** 48.8
barm fellys *sb. pl.* leather aprons, 127.11
(no) barn *pron. phrase* nobody, 121.2
baundoun *sb.* power, 66.8; **bondon**, 142.8
baw bond, *sb.* circlet with bow design, 143.21
bawes *vb. pres. 2 sg.* bend, 144.26
bealte *sb.* beauty, 68.34
bed *vb. see* **bidden**
bedene *see* **bydene**
beet *see* **ben**
beh (him) *vb. pret. 3 sg.* leaned, 68.56
beyn *vb.* redeem, buy 1.32; *pret. 3 sg.* **boute** 4.56; *pp.* **hibotht** 16.60, **hybovt** 15.34
beit *see* **ben**
belde *sb.* comfort, 47.56
bemette *vb. pp.* destined, 33.11
ben *vb.* be; **bene** 13.56, **boe** 15.14, **buen** 66.18; *pres. 1 sg. (neg.)* **nam** 69.36; *pres. 2 sg.* **best** 13.44, **ert** 33.25, **ertow, ertou** (art ǃthou) *(neg.)* **nert** 33.31; *pres. 3 sg.* **his** 3.43, 49, *(neg.)* **nys** 51.8, *(fut.)* **bes** 22.9, *(fut.)* **bese** 46.19, **beet** 42.18; *pres. pl.* **beit** 16.41, **beoth** 47.1; *pret. subj. pl. (neg.)* **nere** 30.7
bende *sb.* bond, 10.35
bene *see* **bone**
bere *sb.* voice, 51.7
bern *sb.* child, 1.13
bern *vb.* bear, 106.7
bes *see* **ben**
besett *vb. pp.* bestowed, 86.43
best *vb. see* **ben**

beste *sb.* creature, 18.5

betacht *vb. pret. 3 sg.* offered, 33.36

bete *vb.* cure, 27.36

bethilge *vb. imp. sg.* make patient, 144.20

bette *vb. pp.* beaten, 50.50

bewent *vb. pp.* wound about, 41.46

bewes *vb. pres. 2 sg.* kiss, 144.25

bicomen *vb.* get to; *pret. sg.* **bycome** 25.15; *pp.* **bicomen** 47.22

bidden, bydden *vb.* ask, pray, entreat, wish, bid, command; *pres. 1 sg.* **byd** 50.17, **bydde** 69.9; *pres. 3 sg.* **bit** 13.26; *pret. 3 sg.* **bahit** 3.18, **bed** 114.19; *imp. sg.* **byd** 50.22

byde *vb. pres. 1 sg.* wait, expect, obtain; 50.17; 69.10

bydene *adv.* forthwith, 30.12; **bedene** 143.17

byes *sb. pl.* rings, 112.24

bigeten *vb.* win; *imp. sg.* **biget** 13.48

byglyde *vb.* overtake, 27.6

bihedde *vb. pret. 1 sg.* protected. 24.8

byhette, byhytte *see* **bihoten**

bihichte *see* **bihoten**

bihoten *vb.* promise; *pret. 3 sg.* **bihichte** 4.18; **byhette** 114.27; **byhytte** 1.12; *pp.* **bihot** 22.22

bileuen *vb.* remain, relinquish; *pret. 3 sg.* 4.54

byll *sb.* letter, note, 89.1

bilof *see* **bileuen**

bynome *vb. pp.* taken away, 36.5

bint. *vb. pres. 3 sg.* binds, 12.5

byrid *vb. pp.* buried, 40.12

byse *vb. imp. sg.* look to, heed, 54.4

byspreynd *vb. pp.* sprinkled, 26.8

bit *see* **bidden**

bytand *vb. pres. part.* biting, 45.2

biteche *vb. pres. 3 sg.* commit, 73.17

biter *adv.* bitterly, 34.6

bityde *vb.* befall, 69.11

bytteris *sb. pl.* bitterns, 132.16

blasterand *vb. pres. part.* raging, 139.17

ble, bleo *sb.* complexion, radiance, 16.24; 67.16

blede *sb.* fruit, 10.27

bledis *vb. pr. 2 sg.* bleedest, 16.43

blewes *see* **blowen**

blynne *vb.* cease, 69.17

blyue *adv.* quickly, 27.48

bloe *adj.* blue, 16.24

blowen *vb.* bloom; *pres. 3 sg.* **bloweth** 17.5, **blewes** 144.9

blwet of allmayn *sb.* almond soup, 132.21

bo, *adj.* both, 3.27

bobbid *vb. pp.* beaten, 82.10

boe *vb. see* **ben**

boeth *vb. pret. 1 sg.* beat 24.18; **boet** 24.34

bogges *sb. pl.* thrusts, thumps (?), 112.7

bold *sb.* dwelling, 10.63

bolled *vb. pret.* swelled, 5.2

bondon *see* **baundoun**

bone *sb.* prayer, boon, 25.14; **bene** 10.7

bord *sb.* table, 68.56

borwe *vb.* ransom, 42.7

boserds *sb. pl.* buzzards, 137.27

boskes *sb.* bushes, 12.13

bosketh *vb. pres. 3 sg.* gets ready, 47.20

bote, boote *sb.* remedy, relief, 10.19; 47.56

boute *see* **beyn**

brakes *sb. pl.* bracken, 136.12

brase *sb.* embrace, 83.23

breme *adj.* bright, 68.17; *adv.* brightly, 67.27

brestes *vb. pres. 3 sg.* bursts, 127.6

bryd *sb.* bird, 64.1

brym *adj.* harsh, 139.17

briste *adj.* = **brihte** bright, 3.24

brok *sb.* use, enjoyment, 46.56.

brol *sb.* child, 33.10

brom *sb.* broom (the shrub), 21.1

brude *see* **burde**

bruys *sb. pl.* brows, 115.10
buen *see* **ben**
bugge *vb.* buy, 73.3
bullys of the see *sb. pl.* seals, 137.13
burd *vb. pt. subj. 3 sg.* ought, 45.12
burde *sb.* girl 68.6; **brude** 142.25
burdus *sb. pl.* frivolities, 114.39
but *prep.* except, without, 39.4; 139.9

careyns *sb. pl.* cadavers, 47.46
carke *vb. pres. 1 sg.* grieve, 68.63
cawtelus *adj.* wily, 139.19
chalonus *sb. pl.* blankets, 114.31
che *pron.* she, 106.16
chel *sb.* shield, 1.60
chelde *adj.* cold, 62.17
chere *sb.* expression, face, 66.15
ches *vb. pret. 3 sg.* chose, 12.68
cheson *see* **enchesun**
chyde *vb.* quarrel, 69.9
chiltinge *sb.* child-bearing, 4.35
(to) clayme, *sb.* in response to a call, 144.24
clepe *vb.* call, 29.20; *pres. 1 sg.* **clepe** 54.3; *pret. 2 sg.* **clepedest** 23.1
clerkis *sb. pl.* scholars, 80.4
clingge *vb. pres. subj. sg.* cling to, 22.8
clyppe *vb. pres. 1 sg.* embrace, 50.71
clogges *sb. pl.* blocks, 112.4
clos *sb.* yard, 111.7
clot[1] *sb.* clod, 22.8
clot[2] *sb.* clout, 114.46; **cloutes** 41.46
cold *vb. pret. 3 sg.* knew, 141.8
contein *vb.* remain, 83.34
cook *sb.* cock, 108.1
coppud *adj.* bad tempered, 114.42
cos, cosse *sb.* kiss, 70.12; 124.4
cost *vb. see* **kunnen,** *vb.*
crabbys sour *sb.* the bitter part of a crab, 137.48
crakit *vb. pret. 3 sg.* uttered, 109.13
croke *sb.* hook, 142.13
croke *vb.* grow bent, 47.50
crouth *sb.* crowd, fiddle, 68.29

crowbys *sb. pl.* corbies, ravens, 137.38
custe *vb. pret. pl.* kissed, 69.23

daiyrewe *sb.* first light of day, 1.9
dayne *sb.* worth, 76.1
dalyaunce *sb.* delight, 89.17
dare *vb. pres. 1 sg.* lurk, 68.64
darf *vb. pret. 1 sg.* dared, 61.3
dawes *sb. pl.* days, 33.32
ded, dede *see* **deth**
dede *sb.* deed, 29.24
deiend *vb. pres. part.* dying, 34.6
die *sb.* day, 142.64
deynte *sb.* pleasure, 47.5
deleth *vb. pres. 3 sg.* separates, 10.10
delf *pret. 3 sg.* dug, 46.1
dereworthe *adj.* precious, 68.23; **dereworthlice** *adv.* affectionately, 68.62
derne *adj.* secret, obscure, dire, 3.7
derne *adv.* deeply, 10.45
deth, det *sb.* death; **ded** 1.15; **det** 63.3; *gen. sg.* **dede** 1.10.
dichte *see* **dihten**
diffade *vb.* fade away, 47.8
dihten *vb.* appoint, ordain, array **dyth** 137.33; *pret. sg.* **dichte** 10.49; *pp.* **dyght** 45.17, **idyht** 36.9, **ydyht** 26.2
dynke *vb. imp. sg.* think, 116.7
dintes *sb. pl.* blows, 34.10; **dyntes** 45.7
discrif *vb.* describe, 83.16
dissavable *adj.* deceitful, 139.3
dysseased *vb. pp.* distressed, 50.52
dystene *vb.* make pale, 99.2
dyth *see* **dihten**
do *vb.* do; *imp. sg.* **do** 29.26; *pret. 3 sg.* **dude** 29.24
done *adj.* dark, murky, 40.1
donketh *vb. pres. pl.* wet, 67.28
dow *sb.* deer, 132.26
do we, do wey *vb. and adv.* stop, give it up, etc.; 12.25, 69.9

dowe *sb.* dove, 107.4
dowel *vb.* dwell, 123.11
dowgit *adj.* obstinate, 139.3
draucht *sb.* inclination, 10.36
dreccheth *vb. pres. 3 sg.* afflicts, 7.21
drede[1] *sb.* dread, 10.29
drede[2] *sb.* doubt, 47.43
dreed *see* **dreie**
dreich *adj.* patient, 10.34
dreie, drye *vb.* suffer, 4.29, 15.45; *pres. 1 sg.* **dree** 54.1; *pres. 3 sg.* **drith** 4.38; *imp. sg.* **drehy** 13.25; *pret. sg.* **dreed** 45.7, **drei** 4.13
drying *sb.* drink, 62.15
droupne *vb. pres. 1 sg.* languish, 68.64
drowryis *sb. pl.* love-tokens, 107.2
duere *adv.* dear, 27.18
dulles *sb. pl.* flat of the hands, slaps (?), 45.7
dur *sb.* deer, 12.59

eche *vb.* increase, 70.11
edi *adj.* blessed, 4.44
(till) eft *adv.* till another time, 144.22
elde *vb.* grow old, 47.50
enchesun *sb.* reason 47.26; **cheson** 114.12
ende *see* **hende** *adj. and sb.*
endre *adj.* (with **dai**) the other day, 22.4
engles *sb. pl.* angels, 10.2
ennuye (the) *vb. pres. 2 sg.* become weary, 47.83
ern, *vb. imp. sg.* procure, 25.12
ernemorwe, *sb.* daybreak, 35.1
ert, ertou, ertow *see* **ben**
eth *adv.* readily, 10.5
eued *see* **heued**
euene *adj.* equal, 41.51
euene *sb.* occasion, 3.16
euene, *sb.* = **heuene** heaven, 4.61
euening *sb.* equal, 10.44
ey *sb.* egg, 107.12
eyses *sb. pl.* comforts, 13.27

eysyl *sb.* vinegar, 24.16

falas *sb.* sophism, 46.53
falewen *vb.* fade, 27.57; *pres. 1 sg.* **falwe** 69.3
fare, fore *sb.* journey, state, practice 7.3; **moder fare** a mother's state 1.44
fehit *see* **fet**
feye *adj.* dying, dead, 66.20
fel *adj. cruel*, 83.9
fele *adv.* much, 67.10
fen *sb.* mud, 68.60
fend, feonde *sb.* enemy; **that fend, the feonde,** the Devil 10.37, 13.31; **uendus,** devils 35.4
fere *sb.* companion, 94.21
ferede *vb. pret. 3 sg.* caused fear in, 28.31
fere flunderys *sb. pl.* sparks of fire, 127.12
ferly *adv.* marvellously, 67.10
fersed *vb. pp.* driven, 143.48
fet *sb. pl.* feet; **fehit** 3.27; **fetd** 15.23
fett *vb.* steal, 105.6
fiele *sb.* viele, fiddle, 68.29
fille *sb.* wild thyme, 67.18
fine *vb.* end, 7.8
fleme *sb.* fugitive, 67.36
flitte *sb.* flight, journey, 7.5
fode *sb.* creature; **vch an fode,** each creature, 28.31
fol *adj.* evil (foul) or foolish; **fol wyman,** i.e. harlots, 7.48
foles *see* **fowel**
fonden *vb.* test, endeavour, 12.35; *imp. sg.* **fonde** 13.45; *pp.* **fonden** 45.21; *adv. phrase* **to fonde,** temptingly, 68.8, 15
fongen *vb.* receive; *pret. 2 sg.* **vonge** 25.5
forborne *vb. pp.* weighted down, 45.12
forcast *vb.* throw over, 144.23

fore *adv.*; **fore care** are anxious about, 39.3

forleten *vb.* forsake, 14.9; **forlete** 16.6

forlore *vb. pp.* lost, 9.19

forthi *conj.* therefor, 46.41

forthrast *vb. infin.* thrust away, 144.19

forwake *vb. pp.* worn out with lack of sleep, 66.31

fowel *sb.* bird, **foul** 66.3; *pl.* **fugheles** 19.2, **fuheles** 15.2, **foweles** 18.1, **foles** 144.33

frale *sb.* = **thrale** (?) bondage, 96.7

fre *adj.* beautiful, 68.8

frith *sb.* woods, 18.1

frount *sb.* forehead, 68.15

froure *sb.* comfort, 10.2

fugheles, fuheles *see* **fowel**

funden *vb.* go, 1.52

furmante *sb.* wheat boiled in milk, 132.25

gabben *vb.* reproach, 3.50

gagil *sb.* crackle, 111.6

garte *vb. pret. 3 sg.* caused, 142.20

gase *see* **gon¹**

gast *sb.* spirit, 46.43

gaste *vb.* ruin, 69.8

geste *sb.* guest 46.67; **gist** 33.31

gewes *sb. pl.* tricks, games (?), 144.3

gy (him) *vb.* conduct his life, 47.35

gyf *see* **yeuen**

gyn *vb. imp. sg.* begin, 24.3

gist *see* **geste**

glawes *sb. pl.* glows, warmth and brightness, 114.4

gleowes *sb. pl.* entertainments, 71.27

glide *vb.* grow sallow, 41.18

gloponed *vb. pp.* startled, 144.4

glosed *vb. pp.* flattered, 129.10

glouus *sb. pl.* gloves, 114.23

gnacchen *vb. pres. pl.* gnash the teeth, 127.9

gome *sb. pl.* men, 144.4

gomenes, gomyn *sb. pl.* games, 71.27; 94.4

gon¹ *vb.* go, 43.5; *pres. 3 sg.* **gase** 46.42

gon² *vb. pret. 1 sg.* began, 27.14

gostly *adj.* spiritual; **gostly syght**, spiritual vision, 50.4

goulinge *sb.* interest, 4.34

graueth *vb. pres. 3 sg.* buries, 30.11

greden *vb.* cry, shout, 3.36 *pres. part.* **gridinde** 34.5; *pres. pl.* **greden** 1.47

grein *sb.* seed, 30.11

greith, greid *vb. imper. sg.* make ready, 64.4

grene *adj.* unripe, 30.11

gret *sb.* high lineage, 108.3

gridind *see* **greden**

gryf *sb.* graft, 106.11

gryffyn *vb.* insert a graft, 106.11

gryht *sb.* security, 25.7

grylle *adj.* severe, 69.34

grysliche *adv.* terribly, 26.2

grome *sb.* anger, 26.11

gronys *vb. pres. pl.* groan, complain, 127.9

grund *sb.* ground, core; *dat. sg.* **herte grunde**, heart's core 1.11

gulte *sb.* guilt, 29.12

gurde *vb. pp.* thrust, 144.3

gurnardys *sb. pl.* gurnet, dragonet (an armed and spined fish), 137.20

ha *pron. 3 sg. fem. see* **hoe**

habbe *see* **hauen**

hafdis *see* **hauen**

haylsed *vb. pret. 1 sg.* said greetings, 141.20

hakkyt *vb. pret. 3 sg.* chopped, 109.17

halewen *sb. pl.* saints, 52.7

(on) haly *adv. phrase* (?) in pious fashion, 142.38

halse *vb.* hug, 110.12

hap *sb.* fortune, 66.9

hard *sb.* hard conditions, 15.16
harmus *sb. pl.* armes, 115.6
hasse *conj.* as, 3.21
hatheles *sb. pl.* nobles, knights, men, 71.24
hauekes *sb. pl.* hawks, 13.2
hauen *vb.* have, 24.12; *pres. 1 sg.* **habbe** 24.1; *pres. 3 sg.* **a** 80.6; *pret. 2 sg.* **hafdis** 16.47
hawes *sb. pl.* cries of 'haw,' 144.8
he *pron. 3 sg. fem. see* **hoe**
he *pron. 3 pl. see* **they**
hef *see* **heuen**
heine *sb. pl.* = **eyen** eyes, 5.3
heke *adv.* = **eke** also, 15.9
hele *sb.* health, 68.58
heltre *sb.* halter, 110.6
hende *adj. and sb.* comely, comely one, 10.33, 64.6; **ende** 7.12
hende *sb.* = **ende** end, 13.60
hendy *adj.* fair, 66.9
hente *vb.* take, 68.57
heonne *adv.* hence, 6.3; **hyne** 83.30
heowe *sb.* appearance, 1.13
heowes *sb. pl.* servants, 71.24
her *adv.* = **er** formerly, 3.24; **are** 46.20
herber *sb.* arbor, 22.14
here *poss. pron 1 pl. see* **we**
heryinge *sb.* praise, 25.25
herken *vb.* incite, 114.7
hernen *vb.* run, 1.17
herre *adv. compar.* higher, 10.59
herrinde *sb.* praise, 3.43
het, hete *see* **hihten**
hethyng *sb.* scorn, 142.3
heued *sb.* head, 4.19; **eued** 15.25
heuen *vb.* raise, rear up; *pret. pl.* **heued** 45.15; *imp. sg.* **hef** 83.31
heuere *adv.* = **euere** forever, 13.21
hewes *vb. pres. 3 sg.* cries out, 144.7
hey *sb.* = **ey** eye, 16.22
hi *pron. see* **I**
hi *pron. see* **they**
hy *pron. see* **I**

hibotht, hybout *see* **beyn**
hic *see* **I**
hidut *vb. pp.* = **idiht** dealt with, 9.35
hihten *vb.* promise; *pres. 1 sg.* **hete** 46.38; *pret. sg.* **hyght** 46.10, **het** 143.4
hyne *adv. see* **heonne**
hyne *sb. pl.* servants, 59.3
hyppers *sb. pl.* hoppers, 59.2
his *vb. see* **ben**
hyt *pron. 3 sg.* it, 15.7
hyth *sb.* height, 137.31
hithe *adj.* = **hihte** precious, high 1.64
hitt *vb. pp.* fulfilled, 46.49
hivel *adv.* = **evel** ill; **hiuel hit may me like,** it suits me ill 16.33
hiyen *vb.* hasten, drive; *imp. sg.* **hye** 27.48; *pp.* **hyed** 45.9
ho *prep. see* **on**
ho *rel. pron.* who, 47.35
hoe, *pron. 3 sg. fem.* she, 3.33; **a** 3.38; **ha** 3.31; **he** 3.21
hoe *pron. 3 pl. see* **they**
hoere *see* **they**
hol, hole, *adj.* unbroken, 4.51, 54
hole *sb.* aperture, 36.7
hombuls *sb. pl.* humbles (edible entrails), 132.26
home *sb.* private place, 106.18
hord *sb.* treasure, 68.57
horre *sb.* corner, 33.27
hoschet *vb. pres. 3 sg.* = **asket** asks, 4.34
hosprynge *sb.* descendant, 50.76
hounderfongen *see* **vnderfonge**
hu *adv.* how; **quu** 1.4; **wu** 4.6; **wou** 21.2
huerte *sb.* heart, 68.42
humbe *adv.* about, busied with, 3.49
hure *poss. pron. 1 pl. see* **we**
hurled *vb. pp.* shoved, 45.4
hutleten *vb. pp.* = **utleten** shed, 4.26
huth *see* **ut**
hyef *see* **yeuen**

I, ic, ich, hi *1 sg. pron.* I; **hi** 1.5; **hic** 15.8; **hy** 1.17; **ic** 1.20; **icche** 22.2; **ich** 6.6; **isch** 73.3; **y** 1.19; **yc** 114.10; etc.

ybenth *vb. pp.* arched, 115.10

iborewe *vb. pp.* redeemed, 11.5

icast *vb. pp.* arranged, 33.32

ych, yche *pron. see* **I**

yche *adj.* each, 99.8

ichot *vb. pres. 1 sig.* = **ich wot** I know, 68.5

ichulle *vb. pres. 1 sg.* I shall, 66.19

ycoyntised *adj.* apparelled, 26.3

idyht, ydyht *see* **dihten**

ieye *sb.* eye, 99.7

ifere *adv.* together, 13.20

yhent *vb. pp.* obtained, 66.9

ihered *vb. pp.* praised, 10.48

ikud *vb. pp.* made known, 47.19

ylent *vb. pp.* bestowed, 66.25

ylyche *adj.* alike, 58.9

ilist *see* **lihten**

ilke *adj.* same, 1.58

ylong *adj.* dependent, 15.10

ymeind *vb. pp.* drenched, 26.7

inaillet *vb. pp.* nailed, 4.24; **ynayled** 15.21

incypyens *sb.* foolishness, 137.15

inderlike *adv.* inwardly, 7.2

into *prep.* with respect to, 47.84

iqueint *vb. pp.* extinguished, 4.12

yraket *vb. pp.* covered over, 56.6

isaucht *vb. pp.* reconciled, 10.40

isch *see* **I**

ysen *vb.* perceive, see; *pres. subj. pl.* **ysoe** 25.23; *imp. sg.* **yse** 32.2

islawe *vb. pp. adj.* slain, 12.59

ysoe *see* **ysen**

ysome *adv.* together, 26.12

isuongen *vb. pp.* flogged, 14.5

ytherled ithurlid *vb. pp.* pierced, 15.23, 3.27

ythouht *vb. pp.* intended, 31.8

itold *vb. pp.* numbered, 33.32

yuuled *vb. pp.* = **yfuled** fouled, 26.13

(mid) iwisse *adv. phrase* surely, 4.47

iyarkid *see* **yarken**

y-yyrned *vb. pp.* longed for, 66.34

iyolde *see* **yielden**

keht *vb. pret. 3 sg.* caught, 142.13

kende *see* **kinde**

kene *adj.* sharpe, 114.42

kenne *vb. pres. 1 sg.* teach, 46.34

kepes (of) *vb. pres. 3 sg.* keeps no account of, 57.4

kinde *sb.* nature, kinship, (good) stock; **kende** 4.32 **kunde** 25.16; **kynd** 64.2; **kynde** 108.5

kyndly *adv.* naturally, 125.2

(no) kinnes *adv. phrase* of no kind, 34.3

kyskys *sb. pl.* kexes, dry stalks, 137.8

kythe *vb.* reveal, 69.21

kleche, *vb. imp. sg.* clutch, 144.31

klepped *vb. pret. sg.* embraced, 142.50

klewes *sb. pl.* round bodies, buttocks (?), 144.31

(bak) klowes *vb. pres. 3 sg.* scratches back, 144.32

knappes *sb. pl.* knobs, 112.13

knauene *sb. gen. pl.* of apprentices, 127.4

knewes *sb. pl.* knees, 144.23

knyten *vb.* bind up; *pp.* 110.4; *imp. sg.* **knet,** hang up 110.6

(on a) knot *sb.* at a time, 109.16

koyntise, *sb.* device, 144.32

kunde *see* **kinde**

kunne *sb.* race, kin, 10.41

kunnen *vb.* know how, can; *pres. 2 sg.* **cost** 69.17; *pres. subj. sg.* **kunne** 10.45

lace *sb.* snare, 99.13

laitis *sb. pl.* manners, 139.5
lape *sb.* sex organ, 113.17; *pl.* **lappes** 112.17
lawing *sb.* laughing, 13.13; **lahynge** 143.49
lay *sb.* faith, doctrine, 12.76
layke *vb.* play, 144.12
layn *sb.* (?) trust, loan (?), 143.30
lawes *sb. pl.* knolls, 144.12
leden *vb. pret. pl.* took their way, 3.35
leese *vb. imp. sg.* let go, 144.27
lef *adj.* precious, dear, 13.39; **leof** 47.91
lefman *sb.* sweetheart, 15.33; **lem-man** 14.2
lele *adj.* faithful, 47.88
lemman *see* **lefman**
lende *sb. pl.* loins, 10.54
lene *vb. imp. sg.* grant, 25.22
lent *vb. pp.* taken away, 66.11
lenten *sb.* spring, 67.1
leome *sb.* light, 3.1
lepers *sb. pl.* leapers, 59.1
leset *vb. pres. 3 sg.* loses, 73.13
lesse *vb.* lessen, 1.59
let, lett *vb.* prevent, stop, 86.45; 105.4
leten *vb.* left, let fall; *pret. 2 sg.* 88.3; *pret. pl.* 45.16
(of) lette *adv.* lately, 77.1
leue *vb.* cease, 50.74
leuene *sb.* flame; **helle leuene** 1.62
leueth *vb. pres. 3 sg.* = **liueth** lives, 26.14
lewes *vb. pres. 3 sg.* warms, 144.11
lhouth *vb. pres. 3 sg.* = **loweth** moos, 17.9
lhude *adv.* loudly, 17.4
li *vb. pres. 1 sg.* tell a lie, 16.57
libben *vb.* live, 22.10
lycyvs *adj.* luscious, 132.20
lycory *sb.* licorice, 115.7
lift *adj.* left, 142.45
lygh *vb.* lie, 82.26; *pres. 3 sg.* **lith** 82.23, **lyis** 40.1

liht, lith *sb.* light; **herte lith,** heart's gleam 4.11
lyhte *sb.* expectation, 68.54
lihten, lithen *vb.* illumine, relieve; *pres. part.* **lyhtand** 45.22; *imp. sg.* **lithe** 4.62; *pp.* **ilist** 3.1
lyis *see* **lygh**
likes ille *vb. pres. 3 sg. and adv.* is displeasing, 67.24
lime *sb.* limb, 64.7
lynne *vb.* cease, 114.33
listen *vb. pres. pl.* like, 144.12
lith *see* **lygh**
loh *vb. pret. 3 sg.* laughed, 66.15
lokyn *vb. pp.* set, 108.9
lomful *adj.* frequent, 20.4
lossum *adj.* lovely, 66.15; *compar.* **lussomore** 68.12
louiye *vb. infin.* love, 10.45
low *sb.* love. 115.18
low *vb. pret. pl.* laughed, 130.4
lowe *sb.* **a lowe,** on a mound 1.27
lud *sb.* language, 66.4
luef *adj. and sb.* = **leof** dear, love; 69.16
lutel *adj., adv.* little, 66.3; **lvtel** 29.1
luther *adj.* evil, 59.3

(with) maistry *sb.* by force, 68.50
make *sb.* mate, 10.60; **mak** 144.36
makeless *adj.* matchless, 79.1
man *sb.* being, person, 1.45
mandeth *vb. pres. 3 sg.* sends forth, 67.16
manest *vb. pp.* threatened, 47.74
marchandie *sb.* merchantry, 31.5
marmsattys *sb. pl.* small monkeys, 137.19
mas *vb. pres. 3 sg.* = **makes** makes, 46.64
maset *vb. pp.* confused, 99.6
maucht *see* **mayen**
may, mey *sb.* maiden, 4.45, 142.13

mayen, may *vb.* be able; *pres. 1 sg.*
  mitti, might I, 1.16; *pres. 2 sg.*
  mith 1.37, **maucht** 10.38, **mittu,**
  might thou, 1.3; *pres. pl.* **moun**
  41.63

maystrise *sb.* mastery, dominion,
  47.18

mawes *sb.* stomach, middle, 144.18

me, *indef. pron.* one, they, 13.26

mede *sb.* mead, 27.32

medel (to) *vb.* occupy oneself with,
  144.36

meene *vb.* remember, 47.61

meyne *vb.* make a declaration, 83.10

mellit *vb. pp.* mixed, 139.21

menen *vb.* lament; **menen mourn-**
  yng, sing a Complaint, 27.14;
  mene 69.4

menget *vb. pres. 3 sg.* mingles, 20.4

menske *sb.* honour, 25.26

mensworne *vb. pp.* perjured, 139.21

menyhe *sb.* attendants, 45.23

mer *sb.* pond, 133.24

merres *vb. pres. 3 sg.* hinders, 46.4

mewes *sb. pl.* haystacks, 144.17

mid *adv.* **mid fare** are concerned
  with, 39.1

myd *prep.* with, 25.17

midsyne *sb.* medecine, 84.28

mihte *sb.* power; **mith** 1.63; **miste**
  3.22

mykel *see* **muchel**

miles *sb. pl.* animals, 67.20

mylsfolnesse *sb.* mercy, 26.20

minde *adj.* in my mind, 1.28

mynges *vb. pres. 3 sg.* remembers,
  144.35

(withoutyn) myse *adv. phrase* un-
  doubtedly, 143.11

misesli *adv.* uncomfortably, 41.47

miste *see* **mihte** *sb.*

mitarst *adv.* now for the first time,
  1.37

mith *sb. see* **mihte**

mythe *vb.* conceal, 69.24

mitti *vb. see* **mayen**

mittu *vb. see* **mayen**

mo *pron.* others, many, 67.22; 86.20

mochil *see* **muchel**

mone *sb.* moan; **make mi mone,**
  sing my Complaint, 16.32; **moone**
  50.39

monĕ *sb.* money, 57.2

monge *vb.* mingle, 68.16

monkunnes *sb. gen. sg.* mankind's
  10.19

moone *see* **mone**

morys *sb. pl.* moors, 137.19

most *sb.* juice of grapes, 26.8

moste *vb. see* **moten**

mostou *vb. see* **moten**

moten *vb.* may, must; *pres. 2 sg.*
  mostou (= **most tou**) 33.2; *pret.*
  subj. 3 sg. **moste** 29.21

muchel *adv.* much, 36.1; **mochil**
  34.14; **mykel** 37.2

mund *sb.;* **hab mund** remember,
  33.15

munde *sb.* dignity, 12.12

munne *vb.* remember, call attention
  to, 29.31; 71.10

murgest *adj. superl.* merriest, 68.27

murgeth *vb. pres. pl.* gladden, 67.20

musketys *sb.* male sparrow-hawks,
  137.48

na *adj.* no, 29.12

nagt *adv.* = **nawiht** not at all, 23.2

nam *see* **bęn**

neb *sb.* face, 3.12

necheth *vb. pres. 3 sg.* draws near, 19.3

nede *adv.* necessarily, 47.39

(but) neid *adv. phrase* needlessly,
  139.13

nelt *see* **willen**

nem *vb. pret. 3 sg.* went, 81.11

nemne *vb.* name, 71.9

ner[1] *adv.* nearer, 70.7

ner[2] *adv.* never, 30.7

nere *vb. see* ben
nert *see* ben
nethere *adv.* downwards, 13.33
neye *adv.* nigh, 16.47
ny *conj.* nor, 51.8
nyd *see* noien
nimen *vb.* take; *imp. sg.* nim 13.41;
  pret. pl. nomen 13.19
nist *sb.* = niht night, 61.1; seuenyst
  week, 62.3
niten *vb.* = ne wite know not; *pres.
  1 sg.* not 41.36, noth 6.4; *pres. 3 sg.*
  nout 29.12
noien *vb.* to be vexed; *pres. 3 sg.*
  nyth 84.5; *pp.* nyd 84.45
noyes *sb. pl.* afflictions, 46.6
noyus *adj.* vexatious, 139.13
nolde *see* willen
noll *sb.* head, 134.19
not, noth, nout *vb. see* niten
nouth *adv.* not, 24.13; nouhth 58.8;
  noust 61.3
nouthe *adv.* now, 24.3
nu *adv.* now, 17.14
nul *vb. pres. 3 sg.* does not want, 29.8
nuste *see* witen¹

o *prep. see* on
offerde *vb. pp.* frightened, 16.16
ohen *vb.* owe, ought; *pres. 1 sg.* ohe
  15.14, ou 14.8; *pret. subj. sg.* othte
  15.28
oht *sb.* oath, 29.18
olod *vb. pp.* dissipated, 46.43
on *prep.* in, on, about; a 12.73; an
  35.1; ho 12.41; o 22.5
onbred *vb. pp.* unsprouted, 107.13
one, on, oon *adj.* one, alone, 1.20,
  26.9, 50.36; won 142.35.
only *adj.* unequalled, 84.8
or *conj.* before, 46.42
ord *sb.* point, 13.46
ore *sb.* grace, 29.14
ostend *vb. imp. sg.* show, 83.20

other *conj.* or, 24.2
othte *see* ohen
ou *see* ohen
ouirlicht *adj.* frivolous, 139.5
ourperte *adj.* impudent, 139.18
ouer *adv.* excessive, 59.1, 2
owwe *adj.* own, 15.14

pay *sb.* satisfaction, 142.26
pappe *sb.* breast, 50.54
paruenke *sb.* periwinkle (the flower),
  68.36
peler *sb.* pillar, 143.48
peryr *sb.* pear-tree, 106.6
pyys *sb. pl.* magpies, 137.29
pyk *vb. infin.* peck at, 132.19
pykys *sb. pl.* pikes (the fish?), 137.12
pine *sb.* torment, 1.35; *pl.* pinis 34.7
pined *vb. pret. 3 sg.* tormented, 1.35
pypy *vb.* pipe, 117.6
pystyl *sb.* epistle, 109.10
pittis *vb. inf.* put, 142.53
planys *see* pleynen
plastre *sb.* poultice, 27.41
pleid *sb.* dispute, 83.15
pleynen *vb.* lament; *pres. 1 sg.* 50.19;
  pres. pl. planys 40.9
plyngyt *vb. pp.* plunged, 121.1
poer *sb.* power, 68.46
porttoryng *sb.* carrying, 132.4
poynt *sb.* lace, tie, 143.27
poyntes *sb. pl.* points, arguments,
  47.93
preue *vb.* try, 47.27
prichte *vb. pret. 3 sg.* pricked, 10.53
prikede *vb. pret. 3 sg.* rode, 114.33
primerole *sb.* primrose, 62.10
pris *sb.* appraisal, value, 3.2
priuey *adj.* secret, 114.22
put *sb.* = pit pit, 8.2

quan *conj.* when, 64.6; quanne 14.1
qwert *sb.* health, 126.8

quyk *adj.* alive, 95.29
quippe *vb. pres. subj. sg.* keep, 123.6
quit *adj.* = **whyt** white, 64.7
qwyt *see* **wyth**
quite *adj.* free from, 4.42
quyten *vb.* pay off, 57.6
quu *see* **hu**

radly *adv.* quickly, 144.14
raght *see* **werche**
raik *vb. imp. sg.* speed, 83.8
rayleth *vb. pres. 3 sg.* puts on, 67.13
rawes *sb. pl.* hedge-rows, 144.14
reaggeth *adj.* shaggy, 114.38
rede *sb.* counsel; **to rede,** as counsel,
   1.34
rede *vb. pres. 1 sg.* advise, 29.13
reysons of corrans *sb.* currants
   (= raisins of Corinth), 132.28
rek *vb.* care, 46.47
relyus *adj.* glittering, 113.19
remeid *vb.* remedy, 83.14
reprevivable *adj.* reprehensible,
   139.18
reulyd *vb. pp.* governed, 125.6
reu *vb. pres. subj. sg.* rob of, 66.33
reuynge *sb.* plundering, 78.3
rewes *vb. pres. 3 sg.* makes feel pity,
   2.2
ryd *sb.* bridle-path, 137.42
rig *sb.* back, 14.5, **ryg** 45.14
rynde *sb.* branch, 107.5
rys *sb.* twig, 40.4
rist *adj.* = **riht** right, 3.3
rode *sb.*[1] rood, cross 1.1; **ruyd** 83.25
rode *sb.*[2] countenance, 2.2; **rude**
   3.14; **rode** rosy countenance, 67.13
rokys *sb. pl.* rooks (birds, or chess-
   men?), 137.20
romnay *sb.* sweet wine, 132.21
ron *vb. pret. 3 sg.* ran, 29.3
ronke *adj.* haughty, 56.7
roow *sb.* roe, 132.27
roun *sb.* counsel, secret, song, speech,
   13.32

route *sb.* crowd, 26.17
(be) rowe *adv.* in turn, 127.15
rowght *vb.* go round, 134.2
rowne *vb.* whisper, 114.21
rowtyn *vb. pres. pl.* crash, 127.15
rude *see* **rode,** *sb.* [2]
ruyd *see* **rode,** *sb.*[1]
rulye *adv.* pitifully, 82.23
rull *vb. pret. 3 sg.* rolled by, passed,
   143.34

sad, sadde *vb. see* **shede**
sade *vb.* be serious, 47.4
sal *see* **schulen**
(in) same *adv.* together, 142.16
sannest *adv.* most suddenly, 47.68
sauen *vb.* save, 64.11
sawe *sb.* say, 41.14
sawes *vb. pres. 3 sg.* shows, presents;
   144.6
se *adv. see* **suo**
secutours *sb. pl.* executors, 46.46
sede *sb.* seed, 10.25
seet *vb. see* **sen**
seete *see* **set**
segges *sb. pl.* men, 144.6
seye *see* **sen**
seien *vb.* say, 13.47
seynorie *sb.* lordship, 31.7
sekkys *sb. pl.* sacks, 137.32
sel *sb.* felicity, 109.11
selde *adv.* seldom, 71.35
seli, selli, sely *sb. and adj.* wonder,
   strange, blessed, 1.24, 25.4
selkud *adj.* strange, 20.1
semavs *sb. pl.* sea-mews, 137.34
semlokest *adj. sb.* loveliest, 66.6
sen *vb.* see; *pres. 1 sg.* **se** 16.2; *pres. 3*
   sg. **seet** *42.17; pret. 2 sg.* **soie** *4.29;*
   pret. subj. sg. **seye** *69.27*
seolcuthliche *adv.* marvellously,
   10.49
seqwens *sb.* sequence book, 81.42
serue *sb. see* **sorwe**
se stoerre *sb.* sea star, 25.1

set *adj.* content, 47.4; **sete** 27.40; **seete** 71.35
sette *vb. subj. sg.* set, 25.7
seuenyst *sb.* week, 62.3
sewen *vb.* follow, pursue; *pres. 3 sg.* **sewes** 144.5; *pp.* **siwed** 68.48
shede *vb.* shed; *pret. 3 sg.* **sadde** 1.65, **sad** 9.42
schef *sb.* creature, 33.8
scenden *vb.* confound, 3.48
scene, shene *adj.* beautiful, 3.12; 69.1
shennesse *sb.* humiliation, 26.23
schent *vb. pp.* discomfited, 42.28
schet *vb. pres. 3 sg.* vanishes, 47.68
schetus *sb. pl.* sheets, 114.31
scille *adv.* plausibly, 69.33
schorte *vb.* be brief, 47.39
shoures *sb.* pains, 27.55
schow *sb.* broth (or stew), 132.19
schroud *sb.* clothing, 26.7
shrudde *vb. pret. 1 sg.* clothed, 24.15
schulen *vb.* shall; *pres. 3 sg.* **sal** 1.34; *pres. pl.* **sylt** 137.49; *pret. 1 sg.* **soldi** (= **solde ic**) 16.28
scumi *vb.* put to shame, 12.29
sich *vb.* sigh, 33.3; *pres. 1 sg.* **siche** 16.31, **sike** 16.1
sykyng *sb.* sighing, 68.44
silit *vb. pres. pl.* = **selleth** sell, 16.57
sylt *see* **schulen**
sinkestou *vb. pres. 2 sg.* singest thou, 22.18
sith *sb. pl.* times, 143.1; **sithe** 143.8; **sythe** 69.23
siwed *see* **sewen**
skaithful *adj.* harmful, 139.11
skald *adj.* abusive, 139.11
skek *vb.* plunder, 46.47
skelk *vb.* mock?, 46.47
skilfuli *adv.* in a reasonable manner, 41.21
skynnge *sb.* glancing covertly, 143.50
skyppers *sb. pl.* skippers, 59.2
slake *vb. pres. 1 sg.* experience a decrease, diminish, 68.67; **slakyn** 78.1

slame *sb.* slime, 46.5
sleght, sleye *adj.* skilful, prudent, 129.11, 16.42
sleythe *sb.* prudence, 78.2
slo, slon *vb.* slay, beat, 68.49, 69,20
smekyd *vb. pp.* blackened by smoke, 127.1
smyt *sb.* smith, 16.42
smulleth *vb. pres. pl.* smell, 27.33
snappes *vb. pres. 3 sg.* nips, 144.2
snartely *adv.* bitterly, 144.1
snelle *adj.* eager, ready, 91.13
snyt *sb.* snipe, 132.17
soht *adj* = **sauch** (OE *salh, sealh?*) pale, sallow, 16.52
soie *see* **sen**
soldi *see* **schulen**
solsecle *sb.* marigold, 68.37
sonde *sb.* serving, 12.40
sore *adv.* bitterly, 66.35
sore *adj.* sorrowful, 142.4
soregh *vb. pres. 1 sg.* sorrow, 19.7
sorwe *sb.* sorrow, 1.55; **sorye** 1.30; **serue** 3.16
sorwel *adj.* sorrowful, 35.4
spakly *adv.* quickly, 142.33
spawyns *sb. pl.* spawns, 137.31
spede *vb.* prosper, 46.2
spel *sb.* speech, 25.5
spil *vb.* destroy, 142.52
spiren *vb.* ask, entreat; *imp. sg.* **spir** 46.2; *pret. 1 sg.* **spered** 142.33
spraulyn *sb. pres. pl.* sprawl, 127.8
stab *vb.* thrust, 45.16
standfra *adj.* aloof, 139.8
stanged *vb. pret. pl.* pierced, 45.11
stark, *adj.* imperious, 27.4
stawes *vb. pres. 3 sg.* is placed (stows), 144.16
steare *vb.* stir, 105.16
stekked, *vb. pp.* fixed in place, 45.16
stelyd *vb. pp.* made of steel, 127.14
steuene, steyuen *sb.* voice, tryst, 3.18, 144.15
stewes *sb.* shed, 144.15

stichte *vb. pret. 3 sg.* stung, 1.53

stide *sb.* place, 144.16

styflyche *adv.* sturdily, 26.4

stille *adv.* softly, 67.21

stokke *sb.* anvil, 127.14

stonden *vb.* stand; *pres. 3 sg.* **stonit,** 16.18

stou *sb.* place, 28.25

stour *adj.* haughty, 27.4

stout *adj.* stately, 68.23

straytly *adv.* tightly, 45.18

streme *sb.* ray (of light), 93.17

streyned *vb. pp.* stretched, 45.18

striketh *vb. pres. 3 sg.* flows, 67.21

strynd *sb.* slope, 144.16

stronde *sb.* stream, 97.3

stunde *sb.* time, moment, occasion; **dede stunde,** moment of death, 1.10; **stoundes** 13.18

sully *adv.* exceedingly, 68.6

swappes *sb. pl.* blows, 112.16

sueteth *vb. pres. 3 sg.* sweetens, grows sweet, 5.5

suetyng *sb.* sweetheart, 68.2

suyes *sb. pl.* sways, 112.25

swik *vb. imper. sg.* cease, 17.14

swylk *adj.* like, 37.3

swyre *sb.* neck, 66.28

swithe *adv.* very quickly, 6.2; **swythe** 81.23

suo, swo *adv.* so, 3.12, 10.14; **se** 16.26

swote *adj.* sweet, 10.21

tabernacle *sb.* wall recess, 50.1

taiclit *vb. pp.* entangled, 139.6

tayled *vb. pp.* entailed, 50.94

take *vb. subj. 3 sg.* accept, 25.14

taries *vb. pres. 3 sg.* puts off, 144.22

tas *vb. pres. 3 sg.* gives, 144.21

tat *dem. pron.* that, 40.10

te *pron. see* **thu**

teyen (him) *vb.* unite, 10.59

tekyl *adj.* exciteable, 110.17

tem *sb.* offspring, 24.20

tene *vb.* grieve, 70.4

tent *sb.* probe, 112.3

terne *adj.* fierce, 139.15

tha *demonst. pron. pl.* they, 45.11

thah *conj.* though, 30.10; **thaiy** 10.61; **thei** 4.39; **they** 13.46; **thaut** 73.7, **thaught** 99.11; **thof** 114.27; **thou** 1.24

thaiy *conj. see* **thah**

that *dem. pron.* those who, 1.38, 39

thaut, thaught *see* **thah**

thawes *sub. pl.* good manners, 144.20

the *pron. see* **thu**

the *vb.* prosper, 33.13

thei, they *conj. see* **thah**

they *pron. 3 pl.*; **he** 12.33, **hoe** 3.37; *gen.* **heore** 10.20, **hoere** 13.4, **hoem** 25.10

then *def. art. acc. sg.* 3.19

thench *vb. imp. sg.* think, 33.14

thewes *sb.* virtues, strength, 10.33; 144.29

thylk *adj.* that, 25.5

thire *dem. pron.* these, 83.8

tho *adv.* then, 1.57

tho *dem. adj. pl.* those, 1.14, 17

thof *see* **thah**

tholen *vb.* suffer, endure; *pres. 1 sg.* **thole** 1.8, **tholi** (= **thole** I) 1.9; *imp. sg.* **thole** 23.4

thore *adv.* there, 41.26

thorit *see* **thurethhut**

thorwgeth *vb. pres. 3 sg.* passes through, 36.8

thou *conj. see* **thah**

thrat *vb. pret. 3 sg.* threatened, 68.49

threpe *sb.* begging, 144.20

threte *vb. pres. subj. sg.* rebuke, 144.29

threwes, thrawes *sb. pl.* twisting, 144.19, 30

throe *adj.* eager, 144.30

throw *sb.* a short space of time, 12.30

thu *pron.* thou; *gen.* **ti** 4.42; *dat.* **the** 1.19, **te** 4.18

thunne *adj.* thin, 29.34
thurethhut *adv.* throughout, 15.4;
 thorit 16.40
thurstungen *vb. pp.* pierced, 1.23
thuster *adj.* dark, 9.24
thwarted *vb. pret. 3 sg.* replied, 82.17
ti *see* thu
til *prep.* to, 83.14; tyll 50.37
titely *adv.* quickly, 142.14
to *conj.* until. 46.16
todrawe *vb. pp.* torn to pieces, 12.58
toened *vb. pp.* injured, 24.2
tollid *vb. pres. 3 sg.* drew forth, 5.2
tonote *vb.* gnaw up, 8.4
torend *vb. pp.* torn to pieces, 3.13
trace *sb.* pæth, 12.55
trace *vb.* track, 137.14
trayling *sb.* trailing of garments,
 13.14
trawes *sb. pl.* truce, 144.22
(tas) treweesse *sb.* makes promises,
 144.21
trye *adj.* excellent, 47.80
trym *adv.* nicely, 113.9
triste *sb.* loyalty, 118.3
troddares *sb. pl.* treaders, 26.8
tunke *sb.* tongue, 21.6

vncouth *adj.* strange, 33.6
vnderfonge *vb.* receive, 81.24;
 hounderfongen 11.10; *pp.* under-
 uon 24.13
underuon *see* vnderfonge
vnlahfulliche *adv.* illegally, 68.54
vnthewes *sb. pl.* vices, weaknesses,
 78.4
unwemmed *pp. adj.* spotless, 10.3
vprace *vb. imp. sg.* uproot, 99.3
uprist *sb.* resurrection, 12.79
ure *sb.* custom, 135.21
ut *adv.* out; huth, 1.18
uallen *see* walle
uendus *see* fend
vergese *sb.* verjuice, 137.48

uerteth *vb. pres. 3 sg.* twists, cavorts
 (?), 17.10 (see commentary)
vichit *see* wiht
viit *see* wiht
vil *sb.* will, 3.43
vise *vb.* devise, 47.14
vo *sb.* foe, 33.19
voket *sb.* advocate, 50.10
vonge *see* fonge
uoryet *vb. pres. 1 sg.* shall forget,
 26.15
vre *adj.* = fre free, noble, 15.27

wai *see* wo
wayted *vb. pp.* spied upon, 69.18
walle *vb.* fall, 12.44; uallen 12.54
wallen *vb.* boil, 12.45
ware *sb.* wares, 74.3
warnyt *vb. pret. 1 sg.* refused, 75.8
washen *vb.* wash; *imp. sg.* wasse 1.14;
 pret. 3 sg. wes 12.63
wat *vb. see* witen *vb.*[1]
waxen *vb.* grow; *pres. 3 sg.* waxit
 16.24; *pres. 3 pl.* waxin 16.8
we *pers. pron. 1 pl.; gen.* here 127.2
 hure 1.60; *acc.* hus 4.64
wede *sb.* garments, 26.2
weene *see* wenen
weete *adj.* wet, 71.33
wegh *sb.* person, woman, 142.17
wel *sb.* = fel skin, 8.3
weldes *vb. pres. 3 sg.* rules, 27.53
wele *sb.* well-being, weal, 45.5;
 weol, 67.35
welkne *sb.* sky, 71.34
welle *sb.* fountain, spring, 10.32
wem *sb.* blemish, 41.27
wenden, *vb.* change, turn, go; *pret.*
 3 sg. went 9.23; *pret. pl.* wende
 4.46; *imp. sg.* went 4.63
wenen *vb.* expect; *pres. 1 sg.* wene
 143.38; *pres. pl.* weene 47.7
weol *see* wele
wepistou *vb. pres. 2 sg.* weepest
 thou, 33.1

werche *vb.* do, create, perform, 11.3 *pret. 3 sg.* **wroth** 33.29; *pp.* **raght** 46.37

werdis *sb. gen. sg.* = **worldes** world's, 43.1

were *sb.* male, 10.50

wernen *vb.* deny, restrain, 1.16; **werne** 9.30

wes *vb. see* **washen**

wey *sb.* way, 25.22

whake *vb.* lie awake, 86.32

whan *adv.* whence, 33.16

whawes, whewes *vb. pres. 3 sg.* moves quickly, 144.27, 28

whe *pron.* we 29.19

whene *sb.* lovely being, 144.27

whyle *adv.* for a time, 66.35

whilen *adv.* formerly, once upon a time, 27.2; **whylen** 69.22

who *sb. see* **wo**

whoder *adv.* = **whider** whither, 33.22

whose *pron.* whoever, 27.7

wyht *adv.* quickly, 67.36

wiht, with *sb.* person, creature, 41.9; **vichit,** the Devil 3.48; **viit,** fairy creature 21.1

wild *sb.* wilderness (?), 33.12

wile¹ *sb.* deceit, 42.12

wile² *sb.* time, 42.15

wylle *sb.* wilfulness, 78.1

willen *vb.* will; *pres. 2 sg. (neg.)* **nelt** 34.15; *pres. 3 sg.* **wol** 28.47; *pret. sg. (neg.)* **nolde** 10.59

win *sb.* bliss; **wnne** 8.6; **wunne** 3.47; **wynne** 25.12; *gen. sg.* **wunne** 67.35, **wynne** 67.11

wynne *vb.* obtain, 69.20

wise *sb.* fashion, manner, 10.24

wyssyng *vb. pres. part.* wishing for, 135.7

wyt, wyth *adj.* white, 114.23; **qwyt** 108.8; **wyt** 117.5

wite *sb.* blame, 142.64

witen *vb.*¹ know; *pres. 1 sg.* **woth** 1.42, **wate** 86.13; *pres. 2 sg.* **wost** 1.44 **wat** 4.49, **wate** 46.35; *pret. 1 sg. (neg.)* **nuste** 68.11; *pret. 2 sg.* **wist** 16.30

witen *vb.*² guard, blame; *pres. 3 sg.* **wyteth** 71.6; *imp. sg.* **with** 1.29, **wyte** 52.3

wyter *adj.* wise, 66.26

wlyteth *vb. pres. pl.* warble, 67.11

wlonk, wlong *adj.* fine, splendid, 12.11

wnne *see* **win**

wo *sb.* woe, 71.28; **wai** 22.9; **who** 71.14

wod, wode *adj.* mad, 3.37, 16.55

wodegare *sb.* forest, 69.31

woderroue *sb.* woodruff, 67.9

wodknyfys *sb. pl.* knives for cutting up game, 137.35

wol *see* **willen**

won *adj.* pale, 66.23

won¹ *sb.* hope, 26.10

won² *sb.* world, dwelling, 68.9

wond *vb.* hesitate, 142.14

wonder *adv.* wonderfully, 29.16

wone *vb.* dwell, 4.65; **won** 45.27

wonges *sb. pl.* cheeks, 29.34

wore *sb.* troubled pool, 66.32

worhliche *adj.* splendid, 68.26

worly *adj.* attractive, 114.17

wortewale *sb.* root of the spur, 108.8

worthen *vb. pp.* become, 3.14

wost *vb. see* **witen,** *vb.*¹

woth *vb. see* **witen,** *vb.*¹

wou *see* **hu**

wowes *vb. pres. pl.* woo, 67.19

wowkis *sb. pl.* weeks, 106.19

wrake *sb.* torment, vengeance, 10.64; **wreche** 13.51

wrathe *vb. pres. sub. sg.* anger, 50.13

wreche¹ *see* **wrake**

wreche² *adj. and sb.* wretched 58.11

wrek *vb. imp. sg.* avenge, 13.42

wrethe *sb.* wrath, 26.11

wriche *sb.* wretch, 99.6

wryed *vb. pp.* accused, 45.5

wrynge *sb.* wine press, 26.8

wroht, wrothe *adj.* angry, 29.16; 111.8

(with) wronge *adv. phrase* wrongly, 71.6

wroth *vb. see* **werche**

wu *adv. see* **hu**

wunne *see* **win**

wurhliche *adj.* splendid, 68.9

yarken *vb.* prepare; *imp. sg.* **yarke** 25.22; *pp.* **iyarkid** 33.2

yate *sb.* gate, 25.4

yef. *conj.* if, 50.59

yeldyng *sb.* paying, 26.15

yern *sb.* yarn, 114.49

yerne *adv.* earnestly, 42.19

yerte *vb. pret. sg.* cried out, 42.19

yeuen *vb.* give; *pres. 1 sg.* **yef** 43.7; *pres. pl.* **yyueth** 112.7; *imp. sg.* **gyf** 46.41, **hyef** 15.42, **yyf** 25.21; *pret. 1 sg.* **yaf** 24.11; *pret. 2 sg.* **youe** 36.4

Iewlye *adv.* in a Jewish fashion (?), 82.24

yftis *sb. pl.* gifts, 89.20

yhe *pron.* = **she** she, 64.7

yielden *vb.* yield, grant; *pres. subj.* **yielde** 4.31; *imp. sg.* **yelde** 13.40; *pp.* **yiolden** 4.40, **iyolde** 36.6

yyf *see* **yeuen**

yongeth *vb. pres. 3 sg.* acts young, 26.4

yore *adv.* for a long time, 66.34

youe *see* **yeuen**

iugeit *vb. pp.* condemned, 139.14

Index of First Lines

Note: This index follows the same alphabetical principles as the glossary.